THE MAKING OF A TEACHER

Teacher Knowledge and Teacher Education

PROFESSIONAL DEVELOPMENT AND PRACTICE SERIES

Ann Lieberman, *Editor*

Building a Professional Culture in Schools
Ann Lieberman, Editor

The Context of Teaching in Secondary Schools: Teachers' Realities
Milbrey W. McLaughlin, Joan E. Talbert,
and Nina Bascia, Editors

Careers in the Classroom: When Teaching Is More Than a Job
Sylvia Mei-Ling Yee

The Making of a Teacher: Teacher Knowledge and Teacher Education
Pamela L. Grossman

The Making of a Teacher

Teacher Knowledge and Teacher Education

Pamela L. Grossman

Teachers College, Columbia University
New York and London

Published by Teachers College Press, 1234 Amsterdam Avenue, New York, NY 10027

Library of Congress Cataloging-in-Publication Data

Grossman, Pamela, Lynn, 1953–
The making of a teacher : teacher knowledge and teacher education / Pamela L. Grossman.
p. cm. — (Professional development and practice series)
Includes bibliographical references and index.
ISBN 0-8077-3047-5 (alk. paper). — ISBN 0-8077-3048-3 (pbk. : alk. paper)
1. English teachers—Training of—United States—Evaluation.
2. English philology—Study and teaching—United States—Evaluation.
3. Teachers—Training of—United States—Evaluation. 4. First year teachers—United States—Case studies. I. Title. II. Series.
PE68.U5G76 1990
420′.71′273—dc20 90-38509
CIP

Printed on acid-free paper

Manufactured in the United States of America

97 96 95 94 93 92 91 90 8 7 6 5 4 3 2 1

Contents

Foreword

The purpose of the Professional Development and Practice Series is to present research, narratives, and descriptions of cutting-edge work that leads to deeper understanding of educational practice and how to improve it. We are at a time of important educational change and need to look to those involved in scholarship who illuminate the complexities of the educational field. Original, fresh insights to age-old problems are needed. Interpretations of, and evidence for or against "glimpses of the obvious" are needed. It is in this genre that the present volume takes its place.

Pamela Grossman makes a major contribution to our field by her penetrating analysis of an age-old problem. How do we educate the neophyte teacher? Is it true that anyone can teach? Is the conventional wisdom correct that one only needs to know a subject well to be a good teacher? Is teaching an art that anyone can intuit? What is the role of higher education in the education of a teacher? Are all methods courses "Mickey Mouse" as many have grown up to believe? How are theory and practice integrated when one actually teaches? What do teachers bring to their teacher education programs? Are alternate routes a viable avenue to creating good teachers? At last we have an important work that begins to question conventional wisdom and, more than that, provides the beginnings of an important set of ideas about the making of a teacher.

By unpacking the phrase "pedagogical content knowledge" we come to understand the differences in what teachers believe and value, how those values get played out in the classroom, and how they impact the treatment of the very content that teachers teach. Six English teachers are the subject of this work. We come to understand them as people and how their beliefs, knowledge, and preparation (or lack of it) affects them as teachers. The myth that teacher preparation makes no difference is exploded in this book but, more importantly, we see why *for the first time*. Grossman explicates the features of a teacher education program that appears to influence some of her subjects as she sensitively describes not only the importance of a coherent vision for teaching and learning for teacher educators who teach subject matter to new students but how the students construct their evolving knowledge and understanding to make it their own.

Perhaps the most pervasive myth in education—that experience is all one needs to become a good teacher—is finally put to the test here. We live with Jake and Megan and the others and begin to understand through the contrast of these six teachers why and how teacher education is important and what influence it has on learning to teach.

This book is a fine contribution to our field. It is beautifully written by an important young scholar who has, at last, shown us how to get at some of the thorny questions that have evaded us for so long. This will surely be the beginning of an important line of work that will have effects on all of us—researchers, teachers, teacher educators, and policy makers alike.

Ann Lieberman
Series Editor

Preface

Efforts to reform teacher education, both past and present, have often focused on limiting or eliminating altogether pedagogical coursework. In the 1960s, James Conant spoke of "those terrible methods courses which waste students' time" (1963, p. 137), while in the 1980s, legislators in Texas severely limited the number of credits in pedagogy allowable for prospective teachers. Many of these reformers have argued that stronger subject matter knowledge and fewer hours spent on pedagogy will create better teachers. As former Secretary of Education William Bennett declared, in asking legislators to allow teachers to forgo formal teacher education, teachers should need to demonstrate evidence only of their knowledge of subject matter, their good character, and their ability to communicate with students in order to teach (Education Secretary Says, 1986).

In the context of this folk wisdom regarding the ineffectiveness of teacher education, researchers on teacher education themselves have bemoaned the lack of evidence concerning the actual content of teacher education and its influence on the development of knowledge and belief among prospective teachers (Feiman-Nemser, 1983; Sarason, Davidson, & Blatt, 1962; Zeichner, 1988). As many have argued, the relationship between professional knowledge and professional education in teaching has been poorly conceptualized. The content and structure of teacher education owe more to historical precedent than to a conceptual understanding of how teachers learn to teach. The question of whether or not beginning teachers actually draw upon the knowledge transmitted through educational psychology courses, foundations courses, or methods courses has troubled thoughtful teacher educators as well as critics of teacher education. Recent work on the question of a knowledge base for teaching (Reynolds, 1989; Shulman, 1987) has provoked the need for further study on the exact nature of the knowledge necessary for teaching and the sources of that knowledge.

Research on teachers' subject matter knowledge (Shulman, 1986a) identified pedagogical content knowledge—the knowledge required to teach specific school subjects—as a central component of secondary-school teachers' knowledge. Logically, subject-specific methods courses are the component of teacher education most likely to help prospective teachers develop pedagogical content knowledge. This logical connection between a body of professional knowledge and one aspect of professional preparation provides a starting point for studying teacher education as a source of teacher knowledge.

The study reported in this book investigated both the nature of pedagogical content knowledge in English among beginning teachers and the role of subject-specific teacher education coursework in contributing to graduates' knowledge and beliefs about teaching English. Like much of the recent research in the area of teacher knowledge, the study used contrasting case studies to investigate the nature and sources of pedagogical content knowledge in English. In order to explore the relationship between professional knowledge and professional education, the contrast in the research focused on three beginning English teachers who entered teaching without professional preparation and three graduates of a fifth-year teacher education program that offered strong subject-specific preparation in English education. In contrasting teachers with and without professional education, the research attempted to understand what value, if any, is added through subject-specific pedagogical coursework when teachers are already well prepared in their subject matter. Through a detailed analysis of the courses most likely to transmit pedagogical content knowledge in English, the research also investigated the content of subject-specific teacher education coursework and how the graduates of the program drew upon this content.

The design of the study, described in detail in Appendix A, included six case studies of beginning English teachers. The case studies focused on the teachers' pedagogical content knowledge of English, drawing upon five structured interviews and classroom observations as data. Interviews included questions about teachers' subject matter backgrounds, their knowledge and beliefs about the purposes for teaching English in secondary school, their knowledge and beliefs concerning students' understanding of English, their curricular knowledge of English, and the sources of this knowledge and belief. Two of the interviews posed tasks that were designed to draw upon teachers' pedagogical content knowledge. In one interview, the teachers read and responded to a common text, "The Death of the Ball Turret Gunner," by Randall Jarrell and talked about how they would teach the poem to high school students; in another interview the teachers planned three hypothetical high school English courses.

The six teachers in this study represent, in many ways, an atypical group of teachers, given reports of the general academic ability of prospective teachers (Kerr, 1983; Schlechty & Vance, 1983). All bright and well educated, they were also well prepared in their subject matter. Four of the six held B.A.'s in literature from prestigious colleges and universities, one was completing his doctorate in literature at a research university, and the sixth had first majored in English and then switched to journalism. While the teachers are clearly not representative, their stories offer the chance to test the assumptions of "the bright person model" of learning to teach (Holmes Group, 1986), which suggests that an intelligent person who is knowledgeable about subject matter has little to gain from pedagogical coursework. The atypicality of the teachers thus becomes theoretically advantageous in studying the sources of knowledge about teaching. Lee Cronbach remarked that in comparing camels and horses, one should find the best example of a horse and the best example of a camel: "We don't take two camels and saw the hump off one of them" (1966, p. 85). By selecting teachers who were more or less equally intelligent and well prepared in their subject matter, we can begin to untangle what, if anything, teacher education can contribute to the process of learning to teach.

The research design also included a case study of the subject-specific component of the fifth-year teacher education program from which three of the teachers graduated. Through observations of the courses and interviews with the professor and supervisors, the study investigated the connection between the content of subject-specific coursework and the pedagogical content knowledge in English held by the graduates. As was true of the teachers themselves, the teacher education program was not representative of teacher education in general. Located in a prestigious research university, the program featured rigorous admission standards and professors who were both outstanding scholars and excellent educators in their fields. The program emphasized the subject-specific nature of secondary-school teaching and required both subject-specific methods courses and electives in the content areas. Again, the atypicality of the program holds theoretical advantages. If, in this strong instance of teacher education, prospective teachers did not acquire pedagogical content knowledge that differentiated them from their peers without teacher education, the case for teacher education coursework as an influential source of knowledge would be weak indeed.

This book serves several purposes. The first purpose is to define and delineate more carefully the nature of pedagogical content knowledge for secondary English. The second and more central purpose is to investigate the relationship between this body of knowledge and the content of subject-specific teacher education coursework. The case studies of all six teachers can inform our understanding of the sources teachers draw upon in constructing their pedagogical content knowledge, as well as the specific contribution of subject-specific teacher preparation. Finally, the case studies of teachers who learn to teach without formal teacher education question the assumptions that subject matter knowledge can suffice as initial professional knowledge for teaching and that classroom experience by itself can serve as teacher education.

Chapter 1 opens with the contrast of two pedagogical treatments of *Hamlet* to introduce the themes of the book. The chapter then provides an overview of pedagogical content knowledge and its potential sources.

Chapters 2 and 3 include the case studies of the six beginning teachers; Chapter 2 contains the cases of the three teachers without professional preparation, while Chapter 3 introduces the three graduates of teacher education. The case studies describe the teachers' backgrounds in English and their entry into teaching, the contexts in which they taught, and their knowledge and beliefs concerning the teaching of English. Each case study ends with several of the themes that characterize the individual teachers.

All names of teachers are pseudonyms, and many potentially identifying details have been deleted to protect their privacy. As a mnemonic device, the teachers without professional education were given names of one syllable, while the graduates of teacher education have names of two or more syllables.

Chapter 4 provides a cross-case analysis of the six teachers' knowledge and beliefs regarding the purposes for teaching secondary-school English, their curricular knowledge, and their knowledge and beliefs about students' understanding of English. This analysis both draws upon the earlier case studies and introduces additional data on these topics.

Chapter 5 opens with a detailed description of the first day of class in Curriculum and Instruction in English. The description introduces a number of themes concerning the content and instruction of the subject-specific methods courses that contributed to the impact on graduates described throughout the chapter. The conclusion of the chapter places this course in the context of several analytic frameworks for thinking about effective teacher education.

Chapter 6 describes the implications of the research for policies, practice, and research regarding teacher education. It concludes with what we can learn from both portraits of the probable and images of the possible in constructing our understanding of the relationship between professional knowledge and professional education.

Acknowledgments

I am among the first to recognize the "limits of individual rationality" in intellectual endeavors. This book would not have been possible without the help of many individuals along the way.

I would first like to express my gratitude to the Spencer Foundation for its support of this research. They provided the gift of time when it was most essential. I would also like to thank the teachers who participated in the research. They took time during their hectic first year of teaching to talk with me and welcomed me into their classrooms. Without their help, this study would not have been possible. I wish them all the best.

I would also like to thank Arthur Applebee, Larry Cuban, and Alfred Grommon for their critical advice and encouragement during the course of the research. They provided not only substantive feedback on this work but wonderful role models as scholars and teachers. I would like to thank Sharon Feiman-Nemser for her long distance contributions to this work. Sarah Biondello at Teachers College Press provided help and advice when it was necessary. I would also like to thank Ann Lieberman for her enthusiastic and always collegial support.

I am especially indebted to Lee Shulman, who welcomed me into the world of educational research and stimulated, advised, challenged, and nurtured me throughout my graduate career. He has taught me much about both how to live and how to work, and I have benefited greatly from his keen insight and unfailingly humane wisdom.

I would also like to thank the friends and colleagues who encouraged me throughout the long process of writing and revising, and never tired of critiquing, commiserating or celebrating: Deborah Ball, Barbara Bennett, Ronda Calef, Nathalie Gehrke, Rachel Hooper, Gail Jensen, Stephen Kerr, Lois Loofbourrow, Walter Parker, Cathy Ringstaff, Jackie Schmidt-Posner, Judy Shulman, Ken Sirotnik, Jacquelyn Tate, Sheila Valencia, Suzanne Wilson, Sam Wineburg, and Peter Zingg. I would especially like to thank Anna Richert, who cheerfully read multiple drafts of this manuscript, providing both valuable critiques and friendship.

I would not have been able to complete this work without the love and support of my family. My brothers and sister remained interested and involved in my work. Tybil and Allan Kahn provided much help throughout this study. My parents, Verle and Moses Grossman, inspired me both to pursue an academic career and to raise a family. Their encouragement and daily help enabled me to juggle my multiple roles and to find joy in the balance.

Finally, I would like to thank my husband, David Kahn, and my children, Benjamin and Rebecca, for their endless patience. Benjamin and Rebecca cheered me on with their enthusiasm and rainbow notes of love. David's steadfast love and support sustained me throughout the time it took to complete this work. I can never thank him enough.

1

A Tale of Two *Hamlets*

Jake and Steven, both beginning English teachers, each decided to teach *Hamlet* to their senior English classes. Jake spent seven weeks on the play. He wanted the students to see the interconnections among the themes of the play and to learn the skills involved in textual analysis or, as Jake put it, *explication de texte*. Jake also wanted his students to understand the "power and beauty" of the play's language. During class, he led the students through the play word by word, focusing particularly on the themes of linguistic reflexivity and the reflexivity of the play. His assignments included an in-class analysis of one soliloquy, memorization and recitation of a soliloquy, a five-page paper on any theme in the play, and a final exam. One of the final exam questions was as follows:

> We spent a lot of time talking about the linguistic complexities of *Hamlet*. Words are constantly mentioned in the play, as are tongue, speech, etc. Write a well-developed paragraph on the importance of language in *Hamlet*. How does Shakespeare play with the language? How does Hamlet use language? How are "words" juxtaposed with "actions"? How does Hamlet use words to act? Generally, why is the theme of language so important in this play?

Although he felt the students never fully appreciated the beauty of the play's language, Jake believed that by the end of the seven weeks they understood the themes of the play.

Steven spent two-and-a-half weeks on the play. He wanted to help his students to see the connection between Hamlet's dilemmas and some of the dilemmas they might face in their own lives, and to pique students' interest in the play and in Shakespeare. Steven began his unit on *Hamlet* without mentioning the play. Instead, he asked students how they might feel if their parents divorced and their mother suddenly started dating another man. After asking students to write about their responses to this situation, Steven "introduced a new wrinkle"; he told the students to imagine that their mother's new boyfriend had taken over their father's job and "there's some talk that he had something to do with the ousting of your dad, and you can't quite prove it, but you sort of get that sense." Again, Steven asked the students to write about how they might feel. After this introduction, Steven asked his students to think about at what point they could imagine themselves killing another human being; the students again wrote about their responses to this question. Up to this point, Steven had not mentioned *Hamlet* by name. In informing the students that they would be reading the play, he tried to connect the two scenarios of divorce and murder to introduce the plot.

> I said, "O.K., now we're going to be reading this book and this book is about this guy and his family breaks up. It's not divorce, but it's sort of a strange set of circumstances, and he's really confused and doesn't know what to do." And so I sprung it on them that it's *Hamlet* and kind of got into it a little bit, and essentially just gave them the plot on a really rough level.

During the unit, Steven showed parts of the videotape of the play, providing students with plot summaries, which they read prior to watching. In discussions of the videotape, Steven tried to move back and forth between the play and the students' own experiences, to "narrow the gap between Hamlet's problem and their problem." During this time, the students never read the play itself. In lieu of a final exam, Steven asked students to write an essay in which they chose a characteristic of Hamlet's and demonstrated how that characteristic existed in people today. Steven asked students to find evidence from the text that would support their arguments. The class spent about a week working on these papers, using class time to work in small groups to brainstorm and share ideas, and to organize and revise their first drafts. By the end of the unit, Steven felt that students responded enthusiastically to the themes regarding the family, although he worried that he had not spent sufficient time on the play itself.

What might account for these radically different treatments of *Hamlet*? One could argue that perhaps Jake had more knowledge of *Hamlet*, but in fact Jake and Steven had similarly strong backgrounds in both English literature in general and Shakespeare in particular. The differences in how Steven and Jake represented *Hamlet* to their students reside less in subject matter knowledge than in their respective preparations for teaching. While Steven and Jake both graduated from prestigious undergraduate institutions with degrees in English, only one of them elected to enroll in teacher education.

While possessing similar knowledge of the play, Jake and Steven knew and believed different things about teaching Shakespeare to high school students. Their knowledge and beliefs concerning the teaching of *Hamlet* had a variety of sources. Both of them had studied Shakespeare in high school and possessed vague memories of how their own teachers had taught certain plays. Both had also studied Shakespeare in more depth during college. Jake and Steven also learned about how students respond to Shakespeare from their actual teaching experience. Only Steven, however, had completed a program of teacher education that included a three-quarter sequence on the teaching of English.

DEFINING TEACHER KNOWLEDGE

The entry of college graduates without professional preparation into teaching reflects the long and heated debate over the value of teacher education. Educators from James Conant (1963) to former Secretary of Education William Bennett have argued that education courses simply keep bright college graduates from entering teaching, and have advocated programs that limit or bypass pedagogical coursework. The underlying assumption of this position suggests that a strong subject matter background and a willingness to teach, in addition to a smattering of generic pedagogical knowledge provided during the first year of teaching, are sufficient preparation for teaching.

Responding to assumptions about the lack of quality of professional education for teachers, policy makers in a number of states, including Texas and New Jersey, have considered proposals to limit severely the number of units allowed for pedagogical coursework within programs of teacher education. Yet, as a number of researchers have argued, these proposals ignore the lack of evidence concerning the impact of professional coursework. As Zeichner comments, "It seems basically unsound to be planning major changes in the landscape of teacher education as we are now, with so little knowledge of what teacher education courses are currently like" (1988, p. 22). His comment echoes earlier cries for more detailed studies of professional education for teachers. As Feiman-Nemser (1983) states,

> It is impossible to understand the impact of preservice preparation without knowing more about what it is like. Sarason (1962) characterized the preparation of teachers as "an unstudied problem" and called for "detailed descriptions of how teachers are actually trained." (p. 156)

Part of what has hindered research on the impact of teacher education has been a lack of conceptualization of the relationship between professional knowledge for teaching and professional education as the vehicle through which prospective teachers acquire this knowledge (Howsam, Corrigan, Denemark, & Nash, 1976; Lanier & Little, 1986). As a report on professional education for teachers (Howsam et al., 1976) states, "If the promise of the teaching profession is to be achieved, we must attend to the processes by which its knowledge base is developed and transmitted" (p. 2).

Past research on teacher education, however, has paid little attention to the articulation between a professional knowledge base and the content of professional education. The fragmentary nature of the typical teacher education curriculum shows little evidence of an underlying knowledge base. While the surface curriculum reflects normative beliefs that teachers need to know something about their subject matter, educational psychology, teaching methods, and the philosophical and social foundations of education, little research exists to illustrate whether and how teachers draw upon this knowledge in classroom practice.

When research on teaching has informed teacher education, the relationship has been prescriptive, focusing on teacher behaviors rather than on teacher knowledge. Teacher educators occasionally have tried to incorporate into teacher education research findings on teacher behaviors that were related to student achievement (Lanier & Little, 1986); the attempts, however, lacked a theoretical framework for understanding both the prior knowledge and beliefs prospective teachers bring with them and the knowledge of subject matter, students, and general pedagogy teachers need to draw upon the research judiciously. As Lanier and Little (1986) conclude,

> The absence of a firm knowledge base for teacher education has led to a long-standing and wide-ranging search for the sort of expertise that would be helpful to the practitioner and at the same time raise the status of teacher education in the academic community. . . . Widespread acceptance of the diverse orientations of research psychologists fostered an instrumental view of research on teaching, a view marked by its concern for linear causal analysis, generalization across teachers, and prescriptions of good practice. . . . This approach has explicitly or implicitly encouraged the idea that the findings of research on teaching could be translated directly into content to be mastered during teacher education. (p. 552)

The shift toward studying teachers' cognitive processes—their thoughts, judgments, decisions, and plans (Shavelson & Stern, 1981; Shulman, 1986b)—moved the field of research on teaching closer to a consideration of the underlying knowledge that informs teachers' plans and decisions. Moving from prescription to description, this body of research investigated how teachers planned or made decisions, leading to models of planning and interactive decision making, rather than specific prescriptions for practice (Clark & Peterson, 1986).

Current research has renewed its efforts to describe and delineate the knowledge base of teaching. A number of models of teacher knowledge are currently being generated by researchers in this field. Elbaz (1983) includes five categories of knowledge in her vision of "practical knowledge": knowledge of self; knowledge of the milieu of teaching; knowledge of subject matter; knowledge of curriculum development; and knowledge of instruction. Leinhardt and Smith (1985) categorize teacher knowledge into subject matter knowledge and knowledge of lesson structure. Researchers at Stanford (Shulman, 1986a, 1987; Wilson, Shulman, & Richert, 1987) define seven categories of teacher knowledge: knowledge of content; knowledge of pedagogy; knowledge of curriculum; knowledge of learners and learning; knowledge of contexts of schooling; pedagogical content knowledge; and knowledge of educational philosophies, goals, and objectives. While researchers differ in their definitions of various components, four general areas of teacher knowledge can be seen as the cornerstones of the emerging work on professional knowledge for teaching: general pedagogical knowledge; subject matter knowledge; pedagogical content knowledge; and knowledge of context (see Figure 1.1).

Figure 1.1. Model of Teacher Knowledge

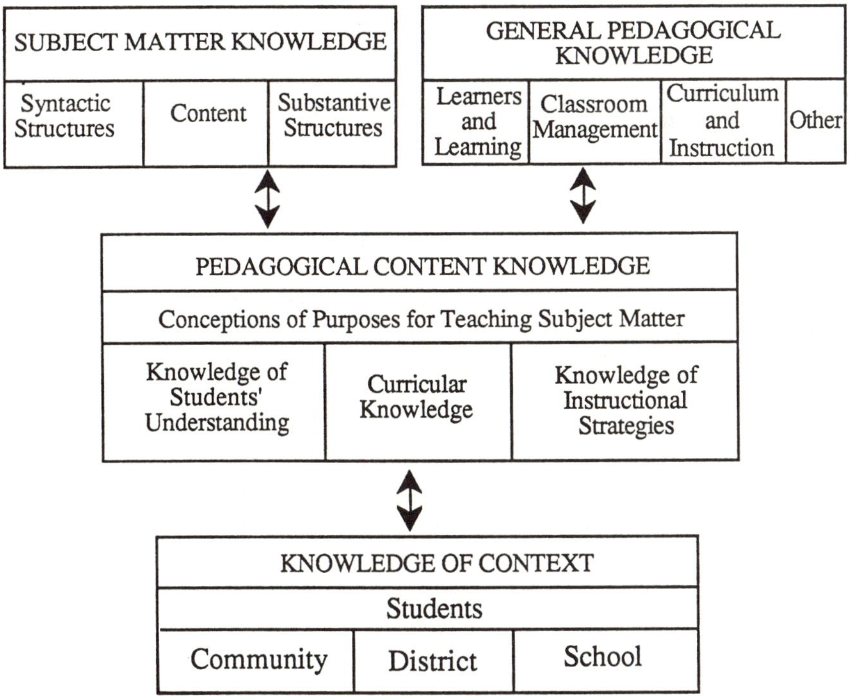

SUBJECT MATTER KNOWLEDGE
Syntactic Structures
Content
Substantive Structures

GENERAL PEDAGOGICAL KNOWLEDGE
Learners and Learning
Classroom Management
Curriculum and Instruction
Other

PEDAGOGICAL CONTENT KNOWLEDGE
Conceptions of Purposes for Teaching Subject Matter
Knowledge of Students' Understanding
Curricular Knowledge
Knowledge of Instructional Strategies

KNOWLEDGE OF CONTEXT
Students
Community
District
School

General Pedagogical Knowledge

General pedagogical knowledge, which has been the focus of most research on teaching, includes a body of general knowledge, beliefs, and skills related to teaching: knowledge and beliefs concerning learning and learners; knowledge of general principles of instruction, such as academic learning time (Carroll, 1963), wait-time (Rowe, 1974) or small-group instruction (Cohen, 1986); knowledge and skills related to classroom management (Doyle, 1986); and knowledge and beliefs about the aims and purposes of education. The historical relationship between research in this area and teacher education has been prescriptive; researchers have identified certain instructional skills related to student achievement that prospective teachers are then trained to use (Gage, 1978). Systems of teacher evaluation that claim to be research-based typically rely on this body of research.

Subject Matter Knowledge

> No man can judge what is good evidence on any particular subject unless he knows that subject well. A lawyer is no better than an old woman at a post-mortem examination. How is he to know the action of a poison? You might as well say that scanning verse will teach you to scan potato crops. [From George Eliot's novel, *Middlemarch*, p. 155]

Subject matter knowledge encompasses another crucial component of the knowledge base for teaching, one that has been ignored until recently (Shulman, 1986a). Earlier studies found little or no relationship between teachers' knowledge of their subjects and student achievement (Byrne, 1983); more recent research, however, has focused on the elements of subject matter knowledge that are important for teaching (Ball, 1988; Grossman, Wilson, & Shulman, 1989; Leinhardt & Smith, 1985; Shulman, 1986a, 1987; Wilson, Shulman, & Richert, 1987). Specific studies have looked at the relationships between subject matter knowledge and classroom questions (Carlsen, 1988; Ringstaff, 1989), critiques of curriculum materials (Hashweh, 1987; Reynolds, Haymore, Ringstaff, & Grossman, 1988; Wilson, 1988), and other processes related to instruction.

Subject matter knowledge includes knowledge of the content of a subject area as well as knowledge of the substantive and syntactic structures of the discipline (Schwab, 1964). Knowledge of content refers to knowledge of the major facts and concepts within a field and the relationships among them. The substantive structures of a discipline refer to the various paradigms within a field that affect both how the field is organized and the questions that guide further inquiry. The syntactic structures of a discipline include an understanding of the canons of evidence and proof within the discipline, or how knowledge claims are evaluated by members of the discipline. (See Grossman, Wilson, & Shulman, 1989, for a further discussion of the components of subject matter knowledge.) The degree to which teachers possess knowledge of substantive and syntactic structures of their fields may influence how they represent their discipline to students (Wilson & Wineburg, 1988). As Kerr (1981) suggests,

> So no matter how skillful one might be in getting students to learn things, the quality of one's teaching depends in important part upon one's understanding the subject well enough both to choose appropriate learnings and to design plans that do not violate the nature of the subject matter. (p. 81)

Without knowledge of the structures of a discipline, teachers may misrepresent both the content and the nature of the discipline itself. Teachers' knowledge of the content to be taught also influences what and how they teach (Shulman & Grossman, 1987). Lack of content knowledge may affect the level of classroom discourse (Carlsen, 1988) or how teachers critique and use textbooks (Hashweh, 1987; Reynolds et al., 1988). Only recently have researchers begun to study how teachers acquire knowledge of particular subject matter during undergraduate studies and teacher preparation.

Pedagogical Content Knowledge

While teachers draw upon both general pedagogical knowledge and knowledge of their subject matters in teaching, research has indicated that teachers also draw upon knowledge that is specific to teaching particular subject matters. Shulman (1986a) terms this body of knowledge pedagogical content knowledge.

> A second kind of content knowledge is pedagogical knowledge, which goes beyond knowledge of the subject matter per se to the dimension of subject matter knowledge for teaching. . . . Within the category of pedagogical content knowledge I include, for the most regularly taught topics in one's subject area, the most useful forms of representations of those ideas, the most powerful analogies, illustrations, examples, explanations, and demonstrations—in a word, ways of representing and formulating the subject that make it comprehensible to others. Pedagogical content knowledge also includes an understanding of what makes the learning of specific topics easy or difficult; the conceptions and preconceptions that students of different ages and backgrounds bring with them to the learning of those most frequently taught topics and lessons. (pp. 9–10)

While the term is new, the concept of pedagogical content knowledge is inherent in Dewey's admonition that teachers must learn to "psychologize" their subject matter for teaching, to rethink disciplinary topics and concepts to make them more accessible to students (Dewey, 1902/1983). In related work, McEwan (1987) describes "pedagogic interpretations," in which teachers interpret specific content in light of what they know about the prior knowledge and interests of students, as the central activity of teachers. Teachers must draw upon both their knowledge of subject matter to select appropriate topics and their knowledge of students' prior knowledge and conceptions to formulate appropriate and provocative representations of the content to be learned. Since the conception of the term, a growing number of studies have investigated pedagogical content knowledge in different subject areas, including social studies and history (Grant, 1987; Gudmundsdottir, 1989; Wilson, 1988), English (Grossman & Gudmundsdottir, 1987; Gudmundsdottir, 1989), math (Carpenter, Fennema, Peterson, & Carey, 1988), and science (Grant, 1987; Hashweh, 1987).

Pedagogical content knowledge, as defined here, is composed of four central components. The first component includes knowledge and beliefs about the purposes for teaching a subject at different grade levels. These overarching conceptions of teaching a subject are reflected in teachers' goals for teaching particular subject matter. Jake, for example, saw the purpose of teaching literature as teaching students the skills of *explication de texte*, while Steven defined the purpose of teaching literature as helping students make connections between a text and their own lives. These two perspectives suggest differing conceptions of teaching literature.

A second component of pedagogical content knowledge includes knowledge of students' understanding, conceptions, and misconceptions of particular topics in a subject matter. To generate appropriate explanations and representations, teachers must have some knowledge about what students already know about a topic and what they are likely to find puzzling. This is implicit in Dewey's notion of psychologizing subject matter and explicit in McEwan's notion of pedagogic interpretations. Research in the area of elementary mathematics has focused on this element of pedagogical content knowledge, as the researchers studied teachers' knowledge of students' strategies for solving different types of problems (Carpenter et al., 1988).

A third component of pedagogical content knowledge—curricular knowledge—includes knowledge of curriculum materials available for teaching particular subject matter, as well as knowledge about both the horizontal and vertical curricula for a subject. For example, English teachers draw upon their knowledge of which books and topics are typically addressed in the ninth grade and how the various strands of a ninth-grade curriculum might be organized. English teachers also draw upon knowledge of what students have studied in the past and what they are likely to study in the future.

A final component of pedagogical content knowledge includes knowledge of instructional strategies and representations for teaching particular topics. Experienced teachers may possess rich repertoires of metaphors, experiments, activities, or explanations that are particularly effective for teaching a particular topic, while beginning teachers are still in the process of developing a repertoire of instructional strategies and representations. Steven's scenario of the disintegration of a family portrays one example of a pedagogical representation of subject matter.

While these components are less distinct in practice than in theory, the concept of pedagogical content knowledge and its parts serves as a useful heuristic for thinking about and studying teacher knowledge. By definition, the concept commits researchers to investigating the content of instruction, thus reintegrating the "lost" paradigm of subject matter into research on teaching (Shulman, 1986a). As research moves more toward accounts of teaching that pay attention to the role of subject matter, pedagogical content knowledge becomes even more salient.

Knowledge of Context

Finally, teachers must draw upon their understanding of the particular contexts in which they teach to adapt their more general knowledge to specific school settings and individual students. Teachers' knowledge, to be of use for classroom practice, must be context-specific (Lampert, 1984); that is, it must be adapted to their specific students and the demands of their districts. Knowledge of context includes: knowledge of the districts in which teachers work, including the opportunities, expectations, and constraints posed by the districts; knowledge of the school setting, including the school "culture," departmental guidelines, and other contextual factors at the school level that affect instruction; and knowledge of specific students and communities, and the students' backgrounds, families, particular strengths, weaknesses, and interests.

While all of these categories of teacher knowledge deserve further research and conceptualization, this discussion focuses on pedagogical content knowledge. If, as a number of scholars have argued (Dewey, 1902; Kerr, 1981; Shulman, 1986a; Wilson, 1988), it is this pedagogical understanding of subject matter that distinguishes between the subject matter expert and the experienced teacher, especially at the secondary-school level, then it becomes important both to conceptualize this body of knowledge in greater detail and to understand its sources. In conceptualizing the articulation between professional knowledge and professional education for teachers, research must also analyze the content of the teacher education curriculum for its potential contribution to the development of pedagogical content knowledge.

DEVELOPING PEDAGOGICAL CONTENT KNOWLEDGE

Teachers have a variety of sources from which to construct their knowledge of teaching a specific subject. As Lortie (1975) suggests, prospective teachers have spent an enormous amount of time in classrooms during their "apprenticeships of observation." Many of teachers' ideas of how to teach particular topics can be traced back to their memories of how their own teachers approached these topics. Teachers also rely on their disciplinary knowledge to shape their knowledge and beliefs about teaching subject matter. Professional education represents another potential source of knowledge. Finally, classroom teaching experience can contribute to the development of pedagogical content knowledge.

Apprenticeship of Observation

Lortie (1975) argues that the time spent as a student provides prospective teachers with images of teaching that prove difficult to overcome. As he points out, the apprenticeship of observation is not a true apprenticeship since the prospective teacher has seen teaching only from the viewpoint of a student. This perspective is likely to give prospective teachers a skewed vision of the nature of teaching (Feiman-Nemser, 1983; Feiman-Nemser & Buchmann, 1985; Lortie, 1975).

The apprenticeship of observation contributes to pedagogical content knowledge in a variety of ways. Experiences as students provide prospective teachers with memories of strategies for teaching specific content. Teachers' knowledge of the content becomes confounded with their knowledge of instructional strategies, since what prospective teachers learned is tied to how they were taught. In this respect, the apprenticeship of observation supports the conservatism of teaching (Cuban, 1984; Lortie, 1975), as teachers replicate the strategies they experienced as students. Because students have more access to teachers' actions than to their goals, these memories are also unlikely to provoke prospective teachers to connect the means of instruction with potential ends.

While Lortie seems to focus particularly on prospective teachers' experiences in elementary and high school, the apprenticeship of observation also encompasses undergraduate coursework. This aspect may be particularly powerful in the development of pedagogical content knowledge for secondary-school teachers. During college, prospective secondary teachers define an academic major and begin more intensive study of the subjects they will later teach. Memories of the strategies used in college classes in a subject may be clearer and more readily accessible than those recalled from high school.

A second relationship between the apprenticeship of observation and pedagogical content knowledge concerns prospective teachers' knowledge of student understanding. Prospective teachers rely on their memories of themselves as students to help shape their own expectations of students (Feiman-Nemser & Buchmann, 1985; Grossman & Richert, 1988). This relationship may be particularly strong, since it takes advantage of the student perspective inherent in the apprenticeship of observation. Prospective teachers may assume that their experiences as students were representative and use their memories of their interests and abilities in a particular subject matter to inform their knowledge of student understanding in that area.

The apprenticeship of observation may also influence prospective teachers' curricular knowledge, since their experience as students exposed them to particular texts and topics in specific sequences at certain grade levels. This relationship may also contribute to the conservatism mentioned by Lortie: Prospective teachers may tend to select curricular materials with which they are most familiar. In relying on their perspectives as students, prospective teachers are likely to remember aspects of the curriculum without knowing the reasons behind their teachers' curricular choices.

Conceptions of teaching a particular subject are unlikely to develop from the apprenticeship of observation. Teachers' goals for teaching a particular subject are less apparent to students than are their instructional strategies and choices of texts and other curriculum materials. The apprenticeship in classrooms may not result in a clear vision of the differing purposes for teaching a school subject. As Lortie (1975) implies, the lack of ends–means thinking inherent in a student perspective on teaching makes a more analytical understanding of teaching difficult to achieve.

> It is improbable that many students learn to see teaching in an ends–means frame or that they normally take an analytic stance toward it. Students are undoubtedly impressed by some teacher actions and not by others, but one would not expect them to view the differences in a pedagogical, explanatory way. What students learn about teaching, then, is intuitive and imitative rather than explicit and analytical; it is based on individual personalities rather than pedagogical principles. (Lortie, 1975, p. 62)

Experiences as English students in secondary and post-secondary classrooms may influence prospective teachers' knowledge of curriculum, their knowledge and assumptions about student understanding, and their repertoire of instructional strategies. Pedagogical content knowledge drawn from the apprenticeship of observation, however, may be more tacit than explicit, more conservative than innovative, and may prove difficult to overcome in professional education.

Disciplinary Background

While somewhat confounded with the experiences through which prospective teachers learn content, knowledge of a discipline also informs the development of pedagogical content knowledge. Decisions about the relative importance of particular content and the selection and sequencing of curricula may have their roots in teachers' subject matter preparation. Some research indicates that beginning teachers' knowledge of their discipline affects their conceptions of what it means to teach a particular subject. Beginning science teachers with graduate work in science, for example, were more likely to believe that a central purpose of secondary-school science is to introduce students to the process of scientific inquiry (Baxter, Richert, & Saylor, 1985), just as math teachers who possessed more knowledge of their subject were more likely to stress conceptual understanding as a goal for students and to emphasize concepts rather than algorithms in the classroom (Steinberg, Marks, & Haymore, 1985).

Teachers' subject matter knowledge may also contribute both to their selection of particular curricula and to their critiques of specific curriculum materials. In one study, science teachers with expertise in physics were unable to identify the central concept in a biology textbook, while the biology teachers could not correct a misconception in the physics chapter (Hashweh, 1987). Teachers who are more confident in their knowledge of subject matter are also more likely to depart from the organization of content found in textbooks (Reynolds et al., 1988). Disciplinary knowledge, then, can contribute both to conceptions of teaching particular subject matter and to curricular knowledge.

In fifth-year programs of teacher education, prospective teachers arrive with knowledge of their subject matter that is distinct from teaching; in four-year programs in which prospective teachers acquire disciplinary knowledge and pedagogical knowledge simultaneously, this distinction may not exist as clearly.

Professional Coursework

While disciplinary knowledge can be acquired in the subject matter strand of teacher education programs, professional coursework also contributes to the development of pedagogical content knowledge. One aspect of professional coursework specifically designed to help students acquire knowledge of teaching particular subject matter is subject-specific methods courses. Theoretically, methods courses are concerned with the knowledge about a subject necessary for teaching it.

> Special methods courses cover selected topics: the structure of the academic discipline, alternative rationales for teaching a subject; the stages and processes of pupils' acquisition of knowledge of that subject; common school curriculum; current trends and innovations in teaching the subject; and specific teaching techniques. (Houston, 1983, p. 1882)

This description of the content of subject-specific methods courses overlaps almost completely with the categories of pedagogical content knowledge. While this component of professional coursework may be the most logical place for prospective teachers to acquire pedagogical content knowledge, we know very little about the content of methods courses or of professional coursework in general. Feiman-Nemser (1983) comments on both the logical connection between professional knowledge and professional coursework, and the lack of research in this area:

> Education courses are the most formal and systematic part of learning to teach. They offer an opportunity to expose future teachers to the knowledge base of the profession. What this knowledge base consists of is unclear. . . . The list of courses that education students take gives some indication of the knowledge presumed to be relevant to teaching. Unfortunately, we know very little about what these courses are like and how future teachers make sense of them. (pp. 154–155)

While Conant (1963) labeled this component of professional education "those terrible methods courses which waste students' time" (p. 137), and others have argued the usefulness of these courses, little empirical evidence exists to support either claim (Zeichner, 1988). Many researchers have argued for more attention to be paid to the actual content of professional coursework in general, and special methods courses in particular. As Zeichner (1988) comments,

> We know very little about what actually goes on inside these courses beyond what students or faculty tell us (e.g., Katz & Raths, 1982) or what foundation sponsored "national studies" have described for us, often based on infrequent and unsystematic "conversations" and observations (e.g., Koerner, 1963). Even the widely acclaimed Conant Report (Conant, 1963) focused more on the number of credits in various areas and on who required them than on the substance of courses. There is no tradition in our field of studying the inner workings of teacher education courses comparable to the enormous amount of work that has been devoted to studying classrooms in the lower schools. (p. 21)

The specific area of English education offers one perspective on the lack of research on teacher education coursework. A systematic survey of a decade of research reported in *Research in the Teaching of English* found that only 3 percent of the articles dealt with the preparation of English teachers (O'Donnell, 1979). As one author concluded, "The relatively meager amount of literature on English teacher preparation is comprised mainly of professionals' statements on how teachers of English *should* be prepared or how they have *not* been prepared" (Quisenberry, 1981, p. 71). Studies that do exist rely primarily on questionnaires sent to professors of English methods courses in various parts of the country, asking for demographic information and self-reports of the content and strategies used in English methods courses (Ganter, 1978; Grunska, 1978; Hipple, 1974; Quisenberry, 1981). Another research strategy involved sending questionnaires to graduates of teacher education programs, asking them for their evaluations of their professional coursework (Fagan & Laine, 1980). One study (Oftedhal, 1985) combined these strategies, sending questionnaires to both professors of English methods courses and practicing English teachers in the Midwest.

The data from these studies are difficult to interpret, given low-return rates ranging from 20 percent to 60 percent and the problems associated with self-report data. In general, the studies offer no clear picture of the content of English methods courses. Perhaps most intriguing are the data on the different perspectives offered by professors and teachers concerning the importance of particular topics for the teaching of English. Oftedahl (1985) found that professors ranked the purposes for teaching literature and composition as important topics, while teachers ranked these topics as low in importance. Teachers stated that methods courses should provide more practical advice and less philosophy of English as a school subject.

In the area of social studies, Katz and Raths (1982) sent a survey to professors of social studies methods courses to collect data on the relationship between the professors' beliefs about the characteristics of competent social studies teachers and the content, goals, and strategies of the social studies methods courses they taught. The study found a lack of correspondence between the professors' goals for the methods courses and their beliefs about the attributes of successful teachers; while the courses focused on knowledge of teaching social studies and general teaching knowledge, the professors believed that teachers were successful less because of their knowledge than because of personal dispositions. The researchers conclude,

> If in fact those attributes of teachers that are associated with successful teaching are *not* addressed in methods classes, and if even the instructors concede that their efforts are directed to goals that are not really important for subsequent teaching success, then there is little wonder that courses have

> little if any impact on graduates' ultimate performance on the job. (Katz & Raths, 1982, p. 14)

Other studies have investigated more directly the relationship between the content or strategies of methods courses and prospective teachers' development of attitudes or knowledge regarding particular content (Lamme & Ross, 1981; Lawrenz & Cohen, 1985; McCaleb, 1979; Smith & Hickman, 1978). Although each of these studies investigates different attitudes, they all assume a link between teachers' beliefs and classroom instruction. Each study also argues that professional courses can influence prospective teachers' attitudes. Implicit in the studies of reading and grammar instruction (Lamme & Ross, 1981; McCaleb, 1979) is the assumption that methods courses can help shape prospective teachers' beliefs about the purposes for studying particular subjects, while Smith and Hickman (1978) argue that a provocative foundations course can alter students' more general beliefs about human nature and teachers. The studies of reading and grammar also illustrate the role of methods courses in introducing innovative practices; both imply that to change traditional practice, professional courses must support changes in attitudes through a variety of interventions. Only the Lamme and Ross study, however, suggests the interrelationship of teachers' prior beliefs and knowledge, the contexts in which they teach, and their response to and implementation of ideas presented in professional coursework. None of the studies discusses the relationship between the specific course studied and the larger program of teacher education.

A number of current research efforts are studying the actual content of teacher education programs in more depth (Feiman-Nemser, 1987; Goodlad, 1988). In their work with the National Center for Research on Teacher Education, Feiman-Nemser and her colleagues are attempting to develop a framework for investigating the influence of teacher education on learning to teach by following students through different programs of professional preparation. In this national study, researchers are studying prospective teachers' prior knowledge and beliefs about teaching, students, and subject matter (Ball, 1988; Feiman-Nemser & Amarel, 1988; Gomez, 1988), and the content and structure of the various preparation programs (Feiman-Nemser, 1987).

Learning from Experience

Finally, teachers acquire pedagogical content knowledge from actual classroom experience. Teaching experience provides the opportunity for prospective teachers to test the knowledge they have acquired from other sources in the crucible of the classroom. Through working with students, they learn about students' misconceptions and prior knowledge of particular topics and about the curriculum (Grossman & Richert, 1988). Teachers also learn what strategies work well for teaching particular topics and the metaphors or representations that are especially effective. While teachers have consistently attributed most of their knowledge to classroom experience (Lanier & Little, 1986; Lortie, 1975), research has also demonstrated some of the "pitfalls" of learning from experience (Feiman-Nemser & Buchmann, 1985). Learning from experience may focus more on "what works" than on overall goals for instruction.

CONCLUSION

Past research suggests at least four possible sources of pedagogical content knowledge: apprenticeship of observation; subject matter knowledge; teacher education; and classroom experience (see Figure 1.2). Each of these sources provides a distinct opportunity for the development of knowledge about teaching English.

Prospective English teachers bring with them to professional preparation their memories of secondary and post-secondary English classes and their knowledge of language, literature, and writing. In the process of learning to teach, they must rethink their disciplinary assumptions about subject matter, as they consider the differing goals and purposes of secondary-school subjects. Methods courses may offer prospective teachers the opportunity to acquire both knowledge about the overarching purposes for teaching a particular subject and knowledge of specific strategies and techniques with which to achieve these larger purposes. Through integration of theory and practice, methods courses can encourage students to engage in the ends–means thinking that may be absent from more purely experiential learning.

These sources of knowledge also interact. For example, if the focus of subject-specific methods courses is on innovative practices, the courses will need to overcome the knowledge and beliefs teachers have already developed through the apprenticeship of observation. If teacher education has had a strong impact, then what teachers learn from subsequent experiences in classrooms may be shaped by prior coursework; if teacher education has been a weak intervention, its lessons are likely to be overwhelmed by classroom experience (Zeichner & Tabachnik, 1981).

This framework suggests that teachers who forgo professional education are likely to rely heavily on both their apprenticeships of observation and their disciplinary backgrounds in constructing their pedagogical content knowledge. Subject matter knowledge may contribute most significantly to conceptions of teaching school subjects, while the apprenticeship of obser-

Figure 1.2. Conceptual Framework

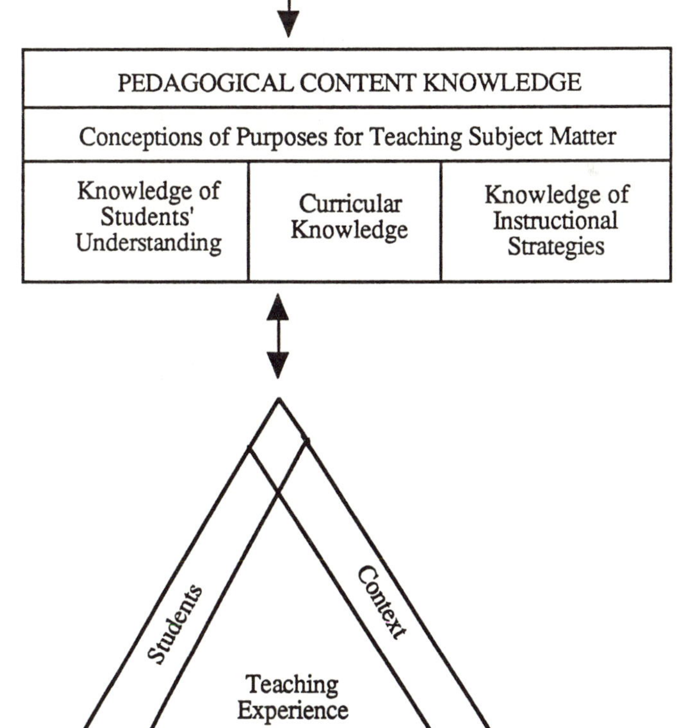

vation may be the source of knowledge of instructional strategies and student understanding.

The six case studies that follow outline the teachers' intellectual biographies and conceptions of English as a discipline, their entry into teaching, their conceptions of teaching English, the contexts in which they taught, and a description of a unit taught by each teacher. The cases focus on both the pedagogical content knowledge of each teacher and the sources for that knowledge.

— 2 —

Learning on the Job

The three teachers discussed in this chapter—Jake, Lance, and Kate—all began teaching without formal teacher education. While Kate had had some prior experience working as a teacher in Japan, Lance and Jake entered the high school classroom directly from college or, in Lance's case, graduate school. These two teachers in particular relied heavily on their disciplinary knowledge of English to inform their pedagogical decisions. Lance, Jake, and Kate all thought back to their own experiences as English students to help them construct their knowledge and beliefs about the teaching of English.

JAKE: AN ENGLISH MAJOR IN THE CLASSROOM

Jake entered teaching fresh from his undergraduate experience as an English major and full of enthusiasm for literature. Although he regarded high school teaching as only an interim job, he looked forward to the opportunity to continue thinking and talking about literature. Jake's experience in the classroom, however, discouraged him, for he was not able to discuss literature at the level he had become accustomed to in college. Appalled by the students' lack of sophistication in dealing with literary texts, Jake concluded that if he wanted to continue teaching, he would have to return to school to obtain a graduate degree so he could teach at the college level. Jake relied primarily on his subject matter knowledge and his experiences as a college English major in constructing his knowledge and beliefs about teaching English.

Intellectual Biography

Jake graduated from a small, elite, liberal arts college with a degree in English. With a father and a brother who were both doctors, Jake initially planned to go to medical school and completed all of the pre-medical requirements, in addition to the requirements for his major. Jake's specialty was twentieth-century literature; his honors thesis was a psychoanalytic study of a twentieth-century novelist. Jake's most memorable professor, who was also his thesis advisor, introduced him to a psychoanalytic approach to the study of literature. Jake found this framework compelling, perhaps because he had toyed with the idea of becoming a psychoanalyst. His favorite English courses were a course in psychoanalysis in literature, a Shakespeare course, and an intensive seminar on Joyce; his favorite writers were Joyce, Kafka, Shakespeare, and Chaucer.

Jake had a passion for literature. As he explained, "I just love reading. I love literature. I had no idea [in college] what it meant to me. Now it really consumes a lot of my life." Seeing English as centered around reading and writing, he believed that "the most important thing for me in literature is not any psychoanalysis, it's not any of that . . . it's *explication de texte*." Jake felt that understanding literature requires strong analytical skills.

> I keep coming back to the word analysis. Analytical skills. Because reading and writing, *explication de texte*, involves grappling with the literature and analyzing it, and seeing how the words make sense and the metaphors and the imagery and the nuances and resonances and all that kind of stuff and then writing about it and talking about it. So I reduce what English is, the way I teach English, to reading and writing.

From Jake's perspective, studying English involves studying a text in great depth, exploring the language and its multiple meanings. He believed adamantly that a text never has a single meaning, relating this idea to Freud's conception of overdetermination.

> Freud's *Interpretation of Dreams* . . . sort of colored my whole view of literature, in that life is overdetermined, literature is overdetermined. You can't be reductive and say, "This is what this means." I don't know how well I teach, but one thing I'll never ever do is say, "This means this." Because that's ridiculous. You don't know literature if you say that.

Although Jake occasionally mentioned what one can learn about oneself through reading literature, this was not his central purpose for the study of literature.

Entry into Teaching

Jake came to teaching in a roundabout way. Although he planned to go to medical school, he reported that he did not have the energy to apply to schools during his senior year of college. As he thought about what to do with himself, he considered teaching: "I needed a job. I like literature and I figured I'd be around it. I knew I couldn't be a college professor yet because I don't have a degree." Jake decided to teach because he loved literature and saw teaching as a way to keep his life centered around literature. As he commented, "because I love literature is why I decided to teach . . . because I like the idea of teaching, of communicating something to someone else, influencing some people, and talking about something I like." Prior to his first year of teaching, Jake was a teaching assistant in a summer program at a private school.

While he enjoyed high school teaching, Jake saw it as an interim occupation, not as a career. Worrying that teaching did not provide enough intellectual stimulation or sufficient opportunity to explore literature in depth, he planned to go on to either graduate school or medical school. As he commented,

> In fact, I don't know exactly what I'm going to do with my life. I will not stay a high school teacher. It's not challenging. I'm very into the literary aspect, and there's only so much you can do with eighth graders, ninth graders, and twelfth graders, no matter how bright they are. . . . It's not enough for me to be gratified by the few students—I think I can reach a lot of the students. I think I'm a good teacher. But I need more personal satisfaction. Meaning, I need kids to inspire me more with literature. You know, rarely does a kid say something about a text that I think is that bright.

Teaching Context

During his first year of teaching, Jake taught at a small, all-boys school run by a religious order. The focus of the school's curriculum was college preparatory; classes were generally very small, with 10 to 15 students per class. Many of the students were from other countries and knew English only as a second language. Jake taught eighth graders, ninth graders, and twelfth graders, in addition to coaching basketball and being responsible for the junior dorm. The curriculum for his courses was generally prescribed by the school, although Jake had some latitude in deciding when to teach certain works or in adding particular units.

Conceptions of Teaching

Jake felt that his conceptions of teaching had changed somewhat as a result of his teaching experience. Prior to teaching, he conceived of teaching as uttering "pearls of wisdom" that students would accept; his experience with his students forced him to rethink this notion.

> I was a little bit more idealistic about it. You know, these are pearls of wisdom coming from my mouth—just take them in. I don't have to do any song and dance. Just sit. No. One, who knows if they're pearls of wisdom and two, that's ridiculous. Especially with eighth graders. And of course, I had no way of knowing that.

During his first year of teaching, Jake came to believe that teaching is essentially entertaining students, trying to get them to "swallow your product."

> Because I think teaching is one hundred percent theatrical. You're entertaining kids—you're an actor. You're making kids swallow your product. I hate to use the term swallow, but you're making the kids buy your product. And some of them don't want to buy your product. They're not interested in your product. So you have to think of different ways to sell your product. . . . Teaching's all acting. If you can act, you can teach. I think you need to be intelligent, but you don't need to be an Albert Einstein to teach.

Conceptions of Teaching English

While Jake saw a number of reasons for teaching English in high school, his central mission centered around his desires to communicate his love of literature and to teach students the skills involved in *explication de texte*. Jake expressed this belief a number of times, in talking about his general goals for teaching, his goals for teaching poetry, and his goals for teaching *Hamlet*. In talking about his overall goal for his students, he commented, "So the biggest thing I can teach you is how to deal with literature there on the page. What do you do when you see it on the page? How do you deal with it? . . . So learn how to deal with *explication de texte*." In talking about his goals for teaching *Hamlet*, he reiterated, "[My major goal for students is] *explication de texte*. To show them how every word is important and to show them how really intricate a play can be." Jake saw poetry as an opportunity for focusing students on the text in front of them and teaching them how to support their ideas with evidence from the text.

> One reason why I like teaching poetry, is . . . it almost forces them to get into the text . . . they come up with an idea which is like totally from Mars, and I say, "show me the word." And they say, "Oh, I dunno, it's just a feeling." A feeling? There are words on the page. This is black and white, they're words. What are the words? . . . So whatever you say the poem's about, support. Show me the words. Show me the language. If you say something, be able to support it, or don't say anything.

Jake's other reasons for teaching English in high school included: English teaches students a way to think; it provides an opportunity for students to appreciate great literature; and literature offers students an opportunity to learn about themselves. Jake believed that teaching students to analyze literature is like teaching math; both require students to think rationally and logically and to engage in "proofs," albeit of different types. He emphasized the importance of teaching classic works to expose students to literature, distinguishing between "valuable" texts, such as classic literature, and what he saw as less valuable popular texts.

While Jake mentioned the opportunity provided by literature to teach students about themselves, he emphasized the other purposes for teaching English, as is evident from his goals for students. His goals included enabling students to write coherent papers with correct grammar and paragraph structure, enabling them to support their ideas with the text, teaching them "to write a lot about a little," making them love literature, and having them see the intrinsic value of great literature. While acknowledging the difficulty of achieving this last goal, Jake emphasized the importance of teaching students to appreciate great works of literature.

> [Students] just have to realize the value of Shakespeare. . . . But it might be hard to convince a kid that *Hamlet* is valuable to read, that Shakespeare is valuable to read. But the teachers should try their hardest. The biggest way I try to convince the students is just because I'm so goddamn enthusiastic about the literature, because I just like it so much. Every time I read *Hamlet*, my God, this is great!

Teaching Shakespeare

In his first year of teaching, Jake taught two Shakespeare plays: *Hamlet* to his senior English class and *The Merchant of Venice* to his freshmen. Both of these plays were part of the required curriculum. While his approaches to teaching the two plays differed somewhat, reflecting the differences in maturity of the two classes of students, the two treatments both followed a word-by-word, in-class analysis of the play and traced themes throughout the play.

Jake reported spending seven weeks teaching *Hamlet* to his seniors; he felt this kind of in-depth analysis was necessary in order to "do it right."

> I spent so long on *Hamlet* because I'm a firm believer in that if you do something you have to do it right. With *Hamlet*, you have to spend time on it, or they won't understand the brilliance of it. You can't just say, "Here's a theme here and here's a theme there." You have to show them how all these scenes are intricate, how they work out in many, many different ways.

Jake's central goals for his students were to have them see the intricate interconnections among the themes and language of the play and to introduce them to the skills of close textual analysis.

According to his reports, Jake ran his classes by going through the play line by line, discussing what was going on in each line. Jake had introduced 10 themes at the beginning of the play, and during discussions the class traced the themes throughout the play. Throughout the discussions, Jake emphasized the linguistic reflexivity of the play, stressing that *Hamlet* was essentially a play about the inability of language to communicate.

While Jake felt that his students generally enjoyed the play and knew it well by the end of seven weeks, he expressed some reservations about their understanding. Once he mentioned he thought they were getting tired of the play; "at the end they were finally getting a little sick of it because we had really gone over it very well. But I think they knew their stuff." Another time he commented,

> I think they really liked [*Hamlet*] and I think they started to see . . . how brilliant in fact it was, just how incredible it was. Some of it, still, I couldn't get through to them as much as I wanted to. Because it's always hard to tell how much they understand. In other words, they can relate things, but do they really understand it? Just the power and beauty of it. . . . It's hard sometimes to get that across.

Jake had many more reservations about teaching *The Merchant of Venice* to his ninth graders. From the outset, he recognized that this class would have a difficult time with Shakespeare, although he was not sure what he could do to make the play more accessible to students. He hoped that at the very least he could introduce them to Shakespeare and have them pick a few themes out of the play.

> What [the students] figure is that if it's hard for them to understand the plot, then it's not worth it. . . . So I'm just trying to give them a basic introduction to Shakespeare and . . . they'll be able to pick out a few themes. And just to see what a play is. In some sense, I'm just really pessimistic about the play.

Jake introduced *Merchant of Venice* with a lecture on Shakespeare and an overview of the different genres; without explicit instruction, Jake commented, the students would assume every work they read was a novel. After this introduction, the class concentrated on the plot of the play and on discussion of a few themes: Elizabethan notions of love, the importance of "bonds" or contracts, and the theme of appearance versus reality. In a typical class, Jake played the audiotape of the play for a minute or two, stopping it to ask students questions about what was happening. Frequently, Jake answered his own questions, as students did not appear to understand the plot. Jake also gave students quizzes on the plot of the play. When the majority of the students failed one quiz, Jake gave them the quiz to complete as homework. When students complained that the play was difficult for them to understand, Jake replied, "These are not mystical questions. I don't ask you the color of Bassanio's hair. If you read [the play], you can answer them. . . . This is English. I'm not asking you to read Greek."

Jake believed that his approach to teaching *The Merchant of Venice* was not representative of his general teaching style. Because the students were encountering so much difficulty, Jake elected, in his words, to spoonfeed them.

> [To teach the play] what I do is I play the tape and we try to go over it. You're seeing such an anomaly because with this play I spoonfeed them and normally I don't spoonfeed. Normally I ask questions, but it takes too long. . . . When I say spoonfeed, I'm saying "This happens in the plot." Then we get to some themes, I'll ask them some questions, but I spoonfeed much more than I ever do.

Jake talked a great deal about the students' difficulties in understanding the play but had relatively few ideas about how to make it more accessible. In general, he blamed the students for being unmotivated and unwilling to work hard to understand Shakespeare.

In addition to quizzes, Jake planned to give a test on *The Merchant of Venice*. He also asked students to do homework assignments related to the play; for example, he asked them to write a paragraph about mercy after reading Portia's famous speech about mercy in the play.

The Influence of Undergraduate Experiences

Jake's ideas about teaching English flowed directly from his knowledge and beliefs about English developed during his undergraduate education. The first indication of this came early on in the interviews, when Jake sorted his college classes according to how they influenced his ideas about English. When asked to re-sort the cards according to how they influenced his ideas about teaching English, Jake maintained that he would sort the cards the same way "because [my college courses] shaped the way I look at literature which helped shape the way I'm going to teach it." He did not distinguish between his conception of English as a discipline and his conception of what it means to teach English in secondary school. He maintained that the model of teaching that worked for him in college, in which eager, motivated students analyzed texts with the help of a professor, was the one he would like to adopt in his own teaching. "But I still would rather teach literature in the way I want to teach it, which is more of the way I was taught. Which is doing *explication de texte*. Which is, when you talk about something, you take plot as a given."

Jake recognized that part of his frustration with his classes stemmed from the difference between teaching and learning in high school and college. While Jake would have preferred to be grappling with texts in a more sophisticated manner, he had to spend a great deal of time motivating and monitoring students, something he found less rewarding.

> College teaching is not high school teaching. . . . In my college, people wanted to learn. That's not the way it is here. That's part of the reason I don't like being a high school teacher. Because that's just not my bag, to make people do their homework. It's like screaming at people to do their homework. That's just not teaching.

For Jake, teaching meant leading discussions about classic literature, asking questions that would enable students to come to some new insights about the work, and sharing his great enthusiasm for literature. The teachers he most admired all shared this enthusiasm for literature and the desire to work closely with a text: "they loved what they were doing. They loved teaching the book. And that's what I love."

Jake's conception of teaching English, then, revolves centrally around literary analysis. In his perspective, the teaching of English involves teaching students to read critically and then to write about literature—the same activities that occupied his time as a college English major. Virtually all of Jake's attributions of the sources for his conceptions of teaching English were related to his undergraduate experience.

Jake's ideas about teaching writing also came from his undergraduate experience. He credited his freshman English teacher with teaching him both how to write and how to teach writing. She corrected papers meticulously, circling every error in red and writing comments that were often longer than the original paper. Jake appreciated her thorough feedback and tried to do the same for his students. "My freshman English teacher [in college] taught me to grade papers like this—not that she knew it at the time—but the way to attack a paper, the way to dissect a paper." Jake also corrected every error he could find in students' papers. Like his college professor, he circled the errors and wrote a one- to three-page summary at the end of each essay, telling students both what they did wrong and what they did right. Yet Jake also recognized a problem with this approach: "Maybe I go overboard. It's possible I do, because sometimes they're just blown away by the red ink. And, like, 'how can I ever learn how to write; this is all red ink.'" Despite his uneasiness with this evidence that his professor's techniques were not as effective with his own students, Jake continued with the same approach.

Difficulties in Acquiring Knowledge of Student Understanding

A persistent theme throughout Jake's interviews and observations concerns his lack of understanding about what makes English difficult for students. While Jake believed he would acquire this knowledge with further classroom experience, he ranked his lack of understanding of student difficulties as the biggest problem he faced as a novice teacher; "As I've said before, it's the biggest problem I have with teaching by far, is trying to get into the mindset of a ninth grader."

Jake found it especially difficult to understand why students encountered problems in reading what he considered to be relatively simple texts. In teaching the story "The Catbird Seat" by James Thurber, Jake was astonished to find that the students did not understand it.

> Some of them read "The Catbird Seat" twice. And they didn't understand a word of it, and that's a fact. I don't know [why they didn't understand it]. I just don't know. And it really upsets me. How could they not understand that? It's just words. I didn't give them *A Portrait of the Artist* to read. . . . This is easy. This is—to me, it's easy. So again, a good teacher also has to have the ability to see things from a teacher's perspective, but also see it from the grade that you are teaching. That there's that perspective. And that's the hardest thing for me to do.

This problem existed from Jake's very first experience at his school. When Jake came to give a lecture as part of his application process, he elected to teach a Kafka story to a ninth-grade class.

> I was practically unintelligible. I mean, they liked me because I was very enthusiastic and clearly knew my material. But what [the search committee] said was the people observing my class got a lot more out of it than the kids did, because of course I never taught ninth graders—I don't remember what I was like in the ninth grade. You forget things. I'm talking about these complex theories and these kids are like, "What?" . . . Some of them, the bright kids, did understand what I was saying.

While Jake tried to think back to his own experiences in high school to determine what would be appropriate for students, he did not really remember what he did in his own high school English classes. Unable to remember his schooldays, Jake relied on his own assessments of the relative difficulty of texts. Jake realized, however, that because of his greater exposure to literature, his undergraduate training, and his greater maturity, his own assessments were likely to be inappropriate for students. As he commented, "It's difficult to know where they're having problems . . . you take for granted how much you know."

Beyond his recognition that students did not have the same knowledge he possessed, Jake seemed unaware of the appropriateness of certain topics for different grade levels. While commenting that students did not know enough to pay attention to the deliberate use of language in literature or to the reflexivity of a text, Jake believed that with training, his students would pay attention to these literary techniques.

> They don't pay attention to the things that someone who's trained in literature should be paying attention to. Like reflexivity. Like the language—they don't really look at the language, why is this word used? So partly it's just training. Learning how to analyze literature is like learning a new language in certain respects.

Jake believed it was his responsibility to provide students with the training necessary for analyzing sophisticated texts, the training he received as an undergraduate English major.

LANCE: THE SCHOLAR AS TEACHER

Having completed all of his coursework toward a doctorate in comparative literature, Lance possessed a more extensive background in literature than any of the other five teachers. A combination of his literary interests and his political beliefs led him to consider the possibility of teaching high school. Lance's disciplinary knowledge and, to a lesser extent, his political beliefs served as the major sources for his ideas about teaching English. During his abbreviated internship in a public school, Lance began to confront some of the disjunctions between his own literary interests and those of his students. Despite his awareness that he would need to rethink his understanding of texts in order to teach them effectively to his students, Lance's disciplinary knowledge seemed to overwhelm his emerging pedagogical instincts.

Intellectual Biography

Lance represents an unusual case for many reasons, chief among them his academic prowess. In two years, Lance earned his undergraduate degree in philosophy from an elite, private university. As a freshman, he enrolled in an interdisciplinary program that combined literature, philosophy, and history in the study of Western civilization. After completing his B.A., Lance immediately enrolled in a master's program in philosophy and literature. After finishing his M.A., he entered a doctoral program in comparative literature.

Lance defined his primary interests as the modern period and critical theories of literature; most of the English courses he had taken centered around literary theory, such as narrative theory or theory of the novel, rather than around a specific period of literature. Lance also wrote fiction and characterized himself as "a novelist intellectual."

Conceptions of English

In discussing the discipline of English, Lance argued that English is composed of literature, grammar, rhetoric, etymology, and the social/historical background to literature. Consistent with this definition, Lance believed that experts in English should possess a "thorough" knowledge of literature, including all of American and British literature through the 1930s; a complete understanding of grammar; knowledge of the history of the English language; and an understanding of American and British history "so they'd be able to contextualize the novels they'd read and also the development of the language."

According to Lance, the study of English revolves around the explication of texts through the tools of literary analysis. Lance found Marxist criticism particularly useful in the analysis of literature. Marxist theory, for Lance, both informed the categories for analyzing literature and identified the themes which make particular books especially valuable. Lance valued both the literary text itself and its historical and social context.

Entry into Teaching

Lance did not set out to become a high school teacher. Rather, the combination of his interest in literature and his political beliefs led him to consider the possibility of teaching high school English after he had rejected the idea of an academic career.

> I knew that I wanted to be an intellectual, that I wanted to be a novelist intellectual. . . . But I don't want to be an academic. I wanted to have some kind of political significance. I wanted to do something. So I decided that I can't teach in a university. That's not going to work for me. But I think teaching is crucial. So I thought maybe at the high school, that would be a level at which I could interfere with the standard systems of normalization and expose students to something that's both

> intellectual, even part of high culture, but that's not co-opted by mass culture and can't be co-opted by just normal systems of power. And I thought, maybe there's a moment for resistance in this. And that's what gave me the idea to teach.

Lance, however, did not want to enter a standard program of teacher preparation, believing that teacher education courses were "too airy-fairy," overly subjective, and not much more than "a rap session." Lance developed these beliefs from talking with friends who were enrolled in teacher education. In investigating alternative routes into teaching, Lance talked with a professor in charge of teacher education at his university and arranged with a local public school to allow him to work as a teaching intern with supervision provided by two experienced teachers at the site. While this was the arrangement under which Lance expected to earn his teaching credential, he later discovered that he had overlooked a number of bureaucratic requirements, including supervision and coursework through an institution of teacher education. Lance was uninterested in pursuing either supervision or coursework. As he commented, "For [the alternative program] you had to have supervision by some other teacher . . . and I had to do some kind of coursework besides what I was just doing in class, and I wasn't interested in doing that either. I just wanted to teach." While the arrangement lasted, Lance taught English and history in a suburban public high school. During this period, he received only nominal supervision from teachers at the school. After several months of teaching, Lance left the school following a disagreement with the administration over his use of controversial materials in his freshman English class.

Conceptions of Teaching

As suggested by his reluctance to enroll in teacher education courses, Lance distinguished between what he termed "the psychology of teaching," which he saw as the basis for teacher education, and just plain teaching; he was interested only in the latter.

> I don't really want to be too much involved in the psychology of teaching, I guess, but rather I just want to teach. I think I don't want to come in with preconceptions about positive reinforcement being necessary, or certain things working as strategies and other things not. But rather, I see teaching more in terms of . . . kind of a Socratic enterprise, in which I do happen to know something about literature, and I do have an approach, but I don't want to be authoritarian in the way I deal with it, and I want to be part of the process and so it would evolve all the time. And that's kind of what I'm looking for.

Seeing teaching as fundamentally a Socratic relationship between teacher and student, Lance believed that there was not much one needed to know about teaching per se, beyond knowing one's subject matter. For Lance, the relationship between teacher and student was more important than specific knowledge about teaching. When asked what he could do to make it easier for students to understand literature that was outside of their experience of the world, he replied,

> I really think that it's kind of dependent on that charismatic element between teacher and student. I think the student has to just trust the teacher . . . if there's a kind of charismatic element and the student somehow bonds to the teacher and is willing to trust the teacher, then I find that he or she will kind of suspend disbelief for just a moment.

Lance wanted as little interference as possible from both administrators and other teachers, stressing his preference for working with students who are interested in learning. "What I want is not to have to deal with bureaucracies but rather just have groups of people who want to learn and to be able to go in there and just teach and talk to them and figure out what they know, and, you know, just do what teachers do."

During his actual teaching experience, Lance resisted all suggestions from both his supervising teachers and administrators at the school. His observations of other teachers convinced him only that he did not want to do what they were doing. Although his one teaching experience did not work out, Lance thought he might be interested in teaching again, as long as he could do pretty much the same thing he had done before. "But I like to have this relationship with people . . . so I really would like to teach. So if it works out and I don't have to do something very different, I really would like to teach."

Conceptions of Teaching English

Lance believed that teaching English involves teaching students to become "incredibly literate" and to engage in critical readings of texts through learning the skills involved in *explication de texte*. Lance's three major goals for students reflect both his ideas about the teaching of English and his political beliefs. The first goal embodies Lance's beliefs about the importance and nature of literacy.

> I wanted them all to be incredibly literate . . . to understand the grammar really well and to be able to use it and by . . . to be literate, I mean rhetoric—to be able to construct arguments, to construct papers that are . . . pretty intelligent, that work . . . and that don't have stylistic or grammatical errors.

Lance's definition of literacy stretches well beyond rudimentary reading and writing.

Lance's second goal for students involves the study of literature. He believed students should be exposed to major works and should learn the skills involved in literary criticism. As he suggested,

> My second goal was to teach them literature. To make sure that they knew certain fundamental texts that they could handle at their age. . . . I wanted to introduce them to the major works of English literature, at least the major authors.

Teaching literature includes teaching students "how to do literary criticism," which for Lance meant teaching "an active view of reading, not just what happened but rather why are these things happening. What's going on in the text."

Lance's final goal for his students suggests the influence of his political beliefs on his conception of teaching English. He wanted students to understand the political and social struggles implicitly embedded in language and explicitly depicted in literature. He saw the study of both language and literature as a way to help his students become more politically aware.

> My third goal was to show them how literature [embodies] social and political struggles and positions, to show them that language isn't just an unbiased medium in which you can do anything at all, but rather it has inherent prejudices in it, and that those relate to a specific historical conjunction. . . . And then also what kind of literature is produced in certain periods and how a canon is constructed, and why some things are included and why other things aren't. And then also, what you can see in literature that gives you a position to resist what's going on and gives you other ways of thinking about your existence, your social existence.

This goal influenced both his teaching of grammar and his curricular decisions about what literature to teach. In talking about how he taught subject/verb agreement in conjunction with a discussion of avoiding sexist language, Lance commented that his students "found my teaching to be not only grammatically rigorous, but also always having a political edge."

Lance believed in the usefulness of organizing the study of literature around particular themes, which often had political significance. For his freshman English class, Lance developed a unit on "marginality and the revolutionary." Since *Animal Farm* was included in the ninth-grade curriculum, Lance decided to begin the unit with this novel. When students found it difficult to analyze the novel using the literary concepts that he was trying to introduce, Lance decided to use the medium of film to introduce categories for literary analysis. Lance showed his students the movie *The Breakfast Club* to help them understand the literary terminology.

> So then I got the idea that if I got something that would be easy for them to consume and also be related to their lives, rather than to class conflict which wasn't too much of an issue in [the wealthy suburb where the school was located], they perhaps would understand better. So I got this movie called *The Breakfast Club* . . . and they did a great job with it. They understood what conflicts were going on, they understood the categories. They were able to understand the categories of literary criticism and how it relates to what's going on.

Following *The Breakfast Club*, Lance wanted to use another, more self-consciously literary film as "a bridge back to literature." His decision to show films illustrates his recognition of the need to connect new topics and concepts to topics or media with which students were already familiar, and highlights the central importance of literary analysis in Lance's conception of teaching English.

Teaching Shakespeare

During his short tenure as a high school teacher, Lance taught *Romeo and Juliet* to his freshman English class. Although it was not his first choice of a Shakespeare play to teach, *Romeo and Juliet* was on the ninth-grade booklist. His class was composed of approximately 25 students, whom Lance divided into "punks, intellectuals, and jock-rahrahs." He characterized the class as untracked, encompassing a wide diversity of ability levels.

Lance mentioned five major goals for teaching *Romeo and Juliet* to his students. His first two goals were to introduce students to Shakespeare and to help them develop an understanding of tragedy, especially Shakespearean tragedy. A third goal involved getting students to understand *Romeo and Juliet*, to appreciate the form of the play, and to memorize specific passages. Lance's fourth goal was to help students develop an appreciation and feel for Shakespearean language. His final goal, which emerged during the course of teaching the play and became his central purpose for the unit, was to help students overcome their phobia about Shakespeare, a phobia he had not realized students brought with them to class.

As Lance had studied Shakespeare in depth, he felt that there was little he needed to do to prepare for teaching the play. In fact, when he first began the unit, he had yet to reread the play because of a lack of time. According to his reports, Lance opened the unit with an introduction to Shakespeare, which included biographical information about the author, comments about the sources Shakespeare had used to write the play, and information about the Globe Theater. In addition, Lance introduced the concept of tragedy, trying to provide a context for the term that encompassed both Greek and Shakespearean tragedy: "I wanted to show them how the chorus operated in Shakespeare as opposed to the Greeks and why the chorus is becoming less and less important and what that meant for Shakespeare."

Although Lance had wanted to preface discussion of the play with a showing of the videotape of the Zefferelli movie of *Romeo and Juliet*, this proved impossible as he could not obtain the videotape in time. Consequently, he asked his students to read the first act of the play at home. When they came to class, he discovered that they hated the play.

> The assignment was for them to read the first act. And they came into class and they all hated it. They hated it. It was horrible. I was really scared. So I said, "Well, let me just start reading the play to you and let's see what happens with it. You know, I'll do like *explication de texte*." And so I started reading it. And I hadn't just read it before class, because I had known Shakespeare pretty well, so I just started reading it in class.

As Lance began reading the play aloud, he saw the comic allusions to sodomy in the first scene for the first time and commented on this use of comedy to the class.

> It surprised me because in class, all of a sudden, I saw this stuff in Shakespeare that I really hadn't seen before . . . but there's these really funny sodomy jokes all through the beginning and so it gets really, really funny. And strange to open up a tragedy with comedy. And so then that led us into this tragedy/comedy thing. I told them about Voltaire and like why Shakespeare represented something really different from what the French or what had gone before, would think of tragedy. And why that really influenced literature later, especially Anglo-American.

In the process of reading the play aloud to the students on the first day, Lance acted it out and showed the class where the actors would be standing. Later, he asked students to act out and direct scenes on their own, an idea he said had come from his own undergraduate course in Shakespeare.

During the course of the unit, Lance said that class time was spent on acting out and discussing scenes from the play and on more general discussions. Lance distinguished between the questions he brought up and the questions the students asked and were interested in discussing. He mentioned that "not everyone was able to deal with the questions I was asking a lot of times," commenting that he focused exclusively on literary topics. The students, on the other hand, were more interested in the plot of the play and more general questions concerning morality and obedience to one's parents. In mentioning this conflict between his own goals and interests and the students' interests, Lance said he was flexible in allowing students to debate the questions they were most interested in, even though their questions were not the ones he found most compelling.

> Just that it was really hard for me to adjust my expectations in the sense that I was always interested in pushing ideas to the extremes, like proving the most obscure theses and showing little nuances in the language that no one had ever seen and why that works. And these kids, of course I know [now], wanted nothing to do with that. That was just totally irrelevant to them. And the whole tragedy bit was really pretty obscure for them. And they just wanted to figure out, like they wanted to get the puns and they wanted to know what was going on . . . like what happened and why it was happening and what it meant. . . . They wanted to know those kinds of things and I guess it was fine. It was hard for me to accept, but then, you know, it's fine.

In addition to discussing the play, Lance required students to learn vocabulary words and to memorize approximately 10 passages from the play.

> And also I made them memorize lots of passages, which they hated. Because I figured they were at an age where they could do it really well. And I think it's good to know, just for itself. They always wondered why I was making them do that. . . . I picked out some really good memorable lines from Shakespeare, and I just wanted them to have a sense of the language, how it worked, how it sounded, how it felt to say . . . and I would make them on a test reproduce it completely, with punctuation and everything, and then explain it afterwards in a second part.

Lance did manage to show the Zefferelli movie later in the unit; in retrospect, he felt it may have only confused the students.

As a final assignment, Lance required students to write an essay about the play. Although he had wanted students to come up with their own paper topics, the students convinced him to assign one. As he had not prepared a topic in advance, he worked one out in class. For the paper, he gave them a quotation—"My only love sprung from my only hate!/Too early seen unknown and known too late!"—and asked students to explain the quotation.

> Do you accept the proposition that it's not coincidental, or an accident, or unfortunate, that the only love comes from the only hate, but because it's the only hate it inspires the only love. . . . Love and hate are seen as the same coin, just two sides of it and how that's the fundamental tragic problem.

In discussing the paper topic, Lance tried to make an analogy between the tragic dilemma in *Romeo and Juliet* and the story of Christ.

> I wanted to show them . . . the solution to tragedy, to the tragic problem, is through sacrifice, and how it's a major paradigm in Western culture . . . not only does it show up in tragedy, but it also shows up in the major religion in Western culture. So that's why I gave them that [analogy]. Because I thought it was interesting that the Christ story works exactly the same way as the Romeo and Juliet story. And I wanted them to see that as a literary technique. They didn't understand it. They just thought I was being pro-Christian, which was not at all the case.

Lance talked at length about the students' performance on the paper. He felt that about a third of the students did well on it, while another third remained at a factual, descriptive level. The final third of the class had chosen to write on their own topics. One student chose to write about why *Romeo and Juliet* was a bad play and should not be taught to ninth graders. After correcting this essay for form and content, Lance wrote "one comment on the paper, like that wasn't what I wanted in the assignment, why that's not valid criticism. In literary criticism, it doesn't make sense to say, 'it's stupid.'" In looking back, Lance said he felt disappointed in the papers because they did not come up with any new or "earth shattering" ideas: "In terms of content, there were no earth shattering ideas that came down . . . and it was a little disappointing for me, but that was just because this was the beginning of my transition from thinking about college to thinking about high school."

In talking about how he might teach the play again, Lance suggested that he would try to rethink the play to come up with a less complex topic for the final papers.

> I would try to rethink the play in a lot more simplistic terms and try to figure out something that had the form of a thesis and paper but that wasn't too complex. What I did was too complex. I'd have to redo it, because that's really hard for me to do. To rethink the play, in terms of simple questions and problems with the text. I mean it would take some work.

Lance could not come up with an alternative paper topic offhand, reiterating that rethinking the play from a less sophisticated point of view would be difficult for him.

The Influence of Subject Matter Knowledge

What is perhaps most striking about Lance is both the strength of his subject matter knowledge and his reliance on his disciplinary knowledge to frame his ideas about teaching. Lance based most of his curricular decisions about texts and materials and the organization of courses on his knowledge of language and literature. His knowledge of literature informed the ways in which he considered organizing a freshman English course in the hypothetical planning interview. While Lance decided to organize the hypothetical course thematically, the themes he chose had their roots in his understanding of literature, rather than any specific understanding of ninth graders.

> Well, I'd probably do two kinds of themes. One is structural themes, like what's a novel, what's a short story, or what's a play and what's a tragedy vs. just any old kind of play. And then also within those broad structural limitations, talk about, well I might even continue more with genres. Like within the novel, different epistolary novels, like eighteenth-century bourgeois novels and early novels, modern novels, stuff like that. I would definitely try to present some kind of huge typology—different genres and structures of literature. And then within that, the themes I would try to pull out would be just either ones that interest me or interested the students. But to do a unit on women's issues . . . I have this tendency to the marginal, so I would also do one with the Black issue. I'd probably do industrialization.

Lance's subject matter knowledge also informed his critiques of curriculum materials. In critiquing a textbook on composition and grammar, Lance criticized the text for not explaining why certain grammatical structures exist in English.

> And so they're both being too rigid in their approach to language and also being really simplistic and therefore making you feel kind of uneasy. Like I bet they use "who" and "whom" and I bet they're not going to explain why it is you do that, even though they go out of their way to talk about it in that way. And so if they don't explain the difference between an inflected and a structural language and like what's going on in the different cases, then I don't think it's really useful to do that.

Lance scrutinized texts for how they represented the subject matter, and judged them on how closely they adhered to what he believed to be important ways of thinking about literature and language. For example, in critiquing a poetry textbook, Lance distinguished between a textbook he felt asked questions that "got students thinking in the right way [by asking] questions which defied platitudes" and a text that asked questions that "promote this kind of bad way of thinking about poetry" by suggesting that students could write the meaning of the poem in a sentence. In critiquing texts, Lance looked for evidence of how they represented both literature and the process of literary analysis.

The dominance of subject matter also appears clearly in Lance's conceptions of what it means to teach English. In many ways, his conceptions of teaching English were practically isomorphic with his knowledge of the subject matter. For example, Lance did not seem to distinguish between his own knowledge and understanding of a text and his goals for teaching that text to students. In teaching *Romeo and Juliet*, Lance's implicit goal seemed to be to help students achieve his own sophisticated understanding of the play. Lance's difficulties in rethinking the play for freshman English also illustrate some of the limitations of learning from experience.

Limitations of Learning from Experience

Without a framework for thinking about how to transform his knowledge of literature for the purposes of teaching, Lance fell back on his subject matter knowledge. The comments Lance made about how he would approach the teaching of *Hamlet* are particularly instructive, as they seem to indicate the difficulty of learning from the experience of teaching *Romeo and Juliet*. In his discussion of how he might teach *Romeo and Juliet* another time, Lance recognized his need to rethink the play from a different perspective. However, in talking about the teaching of *Hamlet*, Lance seemed to have forgotten what he learned about the disjunction between his own literary interests and the interests of students. In talking about how he would teach *Hamlet* to high school seniors, Lance said he would emphasize "sacrifice and mimesis, how structures keep reappearing . . . the early existentialism in *Hamlet* . . . and then the idea of intertextuality within *Hamlet*." His ideas about teaching *Hamlet* show little evidence of rethinking the play from a pedagogical perspective, but mirror the topics he would most like to discuss.

A similar phenomenon occurred when Lance designed a ninth-grade English curriculum. Lance began by talking about organizing the course by both genre and theme. In the midst of developing the themes he might teach,

Lance reminded himself that the students were ninth graders and decided to change the organization of the course. "I'd do just one theme in the course and we'd just read really slowly and we would do the novel, and I would just go chronologically again. And I would bring out who is writing, I would just supplement the information like who's writing, what kind of issues, things like that."

Lance then developed a syllabus around the theme of the development of the novel, which included *Pride and Prejudice, Jane Eyre, My Antonia, The Scarlet Letter, The Adventures of Huckleberry Finn, Great Expectations, Grapes of Wrath, The Sound and the Fury, Animal Farm, Moby Dick, Farewell to Arms*, and *Last of the Mohicans*. When given a choice of novels to add to the booklist, Lance chose *The Apprenticeship of Wilhelm Meister, The Color Purple, The Sorrows of Young Werther*, and *Magic Mountain.*

> If I did *The Color Purple*, I would do *The Sorrows of Young Werther*. And if I did *Wilhelm Meister*, I would decide when I got there, but I would either do something by Thomas Mann, probably *Magic Mountain*, or I would do something like *The Unbearable Lightness of Being* . . . and in doing this, I would like to contextualize all this English stuff between Goethe and Mann and try to show some kind of progression between both the continent and Anglo-American stuff and talk about bildungsroman and what Mann was doing with the modern novel and narrative.

While Lance tried to rethink the organization of the class to make it more accessible to ninth graders, his disciplinary knowledge and interests seemed to overwhelm his emerging pedagogical instincts; he developed a syllabus that includes texts most students do not encounter until college, if at all.

Lance reported learning quite a bit about student understanding of English through his teaching experience. His use of *The Breakfast Club* to introduce literary terms and concepts illustrates one instance of his attempt to rethink the subject matter of literature from an explicitly pedagogical perspective. Yet he did not seem to apply what he learned to the tasks of planning a course or thinking about teaching a text. Lance commented that he saw himself making the transition from college English to high school English, while admitting that he was not quite sure how to rethink *Romeo and Juliet* in order to develop an appropriate paper topic for high school students. Without a clear way to conceptualize high school English and the factors that differentiate it from college English, Lance continued to fall back on his disciplinary knowledge to frame and ground his decisions about teaching.

KATE: FROM THE THEATER TO THE CLASSROOM

As a director of college plays, Kate believed adamantly in the power of theater to transform the audience; her role as a director was to stimulate the audience to see the world differently. As a teacher in a private, college preparatory school, Kate brought into the classroom her beliefs about the power of literature to provide new insights. Seeing directing and teaching as similar pursuits, she hoped to stimulate her students to re-examine their own understanding of life and human nature. Kate believed the subject matter of English offered her the opportunity to expose students to novel ideas and perspectives, while helping students learn to communicate their ideas more effectively. While Kate had no formal teacher education, she had taught English as a second language in Japan for more than a year. In the process of learning to teach English, Kate drew upon her past experiences as a learner, as a director, and as a teacher in a foreign country.

Intellectual Biography

Kate graduated from an Ivy League school with a degree in comparative literature. First intending to major in English, she later switched to comparative literature. She specialized in modern drama and, for her thesis, translated and produced a French play. In addition to her study of French, Kate studied Latin, German, and Japanese.

As a comparative literature major, Kate considered herself well-read in world literature, but somewhat less well read in the classics of English literature; she commented that she had never read Dickens or *Jane Eyre*, for example, and felt weak in poetry. Kate believed she was particularly good at literary analysis and enjoyed looking for metaphors within a text.

Kate did quite a bit of both acting and directing while in college and at first considered a career in drama. She saw theater as a way to reach people, to encourage them to ask new questions about life.

> [My mission in theater] is to encourage transformation in some ways, to make people ask new questions. Maybe they get answers, maybe they don't but to explore their firmest beliefs, to walk out of the theater changed in some ways—feeling new feelings, asking new questions.

Conceptions of English

For Kate, knowing English involves being well-read in different genres and periods and being "well-versed in whatever pool it is that offers the common symbolism that people tap into." She also believed that knowing

English implies a knowledge of language, which to her meant knowing a language other than English. Similarly, Kate maintained that an expert in English would be familiar with literature from other cultures, as well as with literature from the American and British traditions. Knowledge of English also includes an understanding of grammatical terms and structures and mastery of communication skills.

Kate believed that the field of English is composed of literature and spoken language. Under spoken language, she included the structure of language, the history of language, and sociolinguistics. Communication stood at the center of Kate's conception of English. She emphasized that English is primarily a tool for communication, which necessarily includes both verbal and nonverbal communication.

> I tend to substitute communication for English, which brings in all this other stuff. Partially because of my theater background, communication is much more than the spoken word. We've got facial communication, we have body communication, and nonverbal communication.

Kate approached literature looking for what she could learn about the world from the text.

> I'd say I use the text for myself when I'm reading, again like my approach with theater, it's not just a form of diversion or entertainment, but I'm always looking for lessons, that the author has written this with some sort of purpose in mind, and that I'm good at making connections from the text out into life.

Entry into Teaching

Like Jake and Lance, Kate entered teaching in a rather roundabout way. At first she rejected all thought of a teaching career, planning instead a career in theater. The head of the drama department suggested the possibility of teaching, which Kate refused to consider.

> He said, "I think you'd be a good teacher." . . . I didn't want to be rude—he was a teacher—but teaching did not appeal to me at all. I'm embarrassed to say it, but in some ways I guess I viewed it as a lower status position and it was not as glorified as theater . . . but I just never saw myself as a teacher.

Later on, however, Kate began to reconsider the difficulties of a career in the theater and chose to spend a few years teaching English in Japan. She found that for her, teaching and directing were closely related, sharing both a purpose and a style. She saw her mission in teaching as closely linked to her mission in the theater.

> I found to my astonishment that I was using the exact same constellation of skills and talents that I had developed in theater and that had attracted me to theater, but I was doing—accomplishing the same things much more effectively in the classroom. . . . So in the classroom you're doing the same things. You're probing people, you're trying to bring out the best in people. . . . What I was doing with my actors, I now get to do with my students. And it is a question of not telling them, not imposing something on them, but stimulating them in such a way that they do it themselves.

After two years in Japan, during which she taught English as a Second Language to students who ranged from children to adults, Kate returned to the United States to teach English in an independent school.

Conceptions of Teaching

Kate conceived of teaching as a process of stimulation designed to help students achieve new insights about themselves and their world.

> So stimulating, stimulating, stimulating. And helping them to channel whatever is the result of that stimulation into a way that is effective in the world, whether that be in the form of writing or in communicating with words, or into actions, using that knowledge or insight in some way, that's not only beneficial to them personally but beneficial to the world in some way.

In this conception of teaching, Kate saw the role of the teacher as providing materials and questions as stimuli and then probing students for their reactions.

Kate preferred to work with students who were motivated and excited about learning. In talking about how she might teach *A Midsummer Night's Dream* to a hypothetical class of 20 to 25 non-college bound students, she commented,

> That's a really hard question because I honestly don't think I would be teaching in that kind of environment. What I love about teaching would not be there. I love working with kids who are interested in learning. I'm not trying to push so much. I'm there to continue to stimulate.

Kate never seriously considered teaching in public schools because she had heard from friends who were public school teachers that they did not get to teach what they wanted to teach and that they had to concentrate too much on matters of discipline rather than matters of content.

Conceptions of Teaching English

Although Kate loved literature, she saw the teaching of literature as a springboard for discussing ideas that go well beyond the text. Her overall goals for students illustrate Kate's desire to reach beyond the discipline of English.

> My goals for students. It definitely goes beyond just English. They're human beings that I have some kind of responsibility towards. . . . I am potentially a role model for some of them. And it's wrong of me also not to share other things that I've learned in my lifetime. . . . English can be used as a springboard for other things, which I think are important in life. Using the literature as a springboard to look at questions of social responsibility, for example.

Kate saw a number of purposes for studying English.

> One, the kids do learn how to develop analytical skills, which is very important in our culture. And they learn to communicate effectively, again a very important thing. They expose themselves to something which can enrich their lives. And focus on questions which maybe the everyday world does not raise, but people who have stopped and looked at the world from a different perspective and they're sharing whatever insights they had. . . . There's always the obligation of a high school to prepare a student for college and they will have to know how to write. They will have to know how to argue, how to defend their points of view. They have to learn how to back up what they say, how to be specific. . . . So learning how to develop all of these skills. One is developing skills that are necessary and another is opening themselves up to the things that will enrich their lives.

Kate's conception of the teaching of English embodied both a practical and a social mission. Seeing the subject matter as a vehicle both for teaching necessary skills and for fostering self-awareness, she reflects two traditions in the teaching of English—the nonacademic tradition and the classical model (Applebee, 1974). The nonacademic tradition emphasizes the importance of literature in students' lives outside of school, while the classical model stresses the importance of studying English to develop "mental discipline." The nonacademic tradition characterizes Kate's approach to the teaching of literature, while the classical tradition undergirds her ideas about teaching grammar, which focused on the need for students to learn "impeccability" through the study of grammar. As she commented, "Right now I'm teaching a lot of grammar, so I'm using that as an opportunity to introduce them to what it means to be impeccable about something."

Kate saw the teaching of literature, writing, and grammar as distinct and unrelated aspects of the teaching of English. She used grammar as an opportunity to teach intellectual discipline.

> I can see several reasons [for studying grammar]. One is that they're learning an intellectual discipline. It's also providing a tool for the teachers to be able to communicate with the students . . . in a way that supports the students' writing. And the last reason that I can see is that for foreign language teachers. . . . I think it's going to be a real support for foreign language teachers.

Kate's ideas about the teaching of writing were strongly influenced by a friend who had attended a number of workshops on the teaching of writing. This friend lent Kate a copy of Peter Elbow's book *Writing with Power* and shared her new knowledge about teaching writing as a process. Kate observed that her own ideas about the nature of writing underwent a change as a result of the interchange with her friend.

> I used to think that writing consisted of taking your thoughts, which are already there, and putting them there. And I'm learning that those are not distinct processes. That writing creates thought. So the more I write, the more I find out what I think. That writing can be a form of exploration. . . . [My friend] had taken courses on how to teach writing, and it's gotten her extremely excited about it. I envy her tremendously for this. I would love to. I don't feel trained to do all the things I'm doing, and I've learned from her.

Teaching Context

The school at which Kate taught combined a college preparatory curriculum with features of an alternative school; students were given a fair amount of responsibility for their own education and concentrated on only a few courses at a time. The school year was broken up into "blocks" of five weeks, and during each block a student took three or four courses. Classes usually met for concentrated periods of time; at least one day a week, classes met for a longer period. Many of the students chose this school because it welcomed unconventional students. As a group, the students were bright and highly motivated.

During her first year of teaching, Kate taught the freshman English course for most of the year and taught two junior-senior elective classes, including a Shakespeare course. In addition, she taught drama.

Teaching *A Midsummer Night's Dream*

Kate taught *A Midsummer Night's Dream* to her freshman English class, which was composed of 10 students. Her choice of this play was influenced by the fact that the school was putting on the play as its spring production. Her students begged to have the chance to read Shakespeare and were delighted at the opportunity to read the play.

Kate's primary goal in teaching the play was to help students find a way to enjoy Shakespeare. Acknowledging that her students were unusually appreciative of the beauty of Shakespearean language, Kate also believed that *A Midsummer Night's Dream* would appeal particularly to teenagers. "It's so suitable for teenagers, jumping in and out of love, and dealing with emotions and confusion and identity crisis and constantly changing love objects—and so we often would stop and find some ways of relating it to their own lives."

In formulating both her goals and her approach to the play, Kate thought back to her own dislike of Shakespeare in high school, wondering, "How can I make it accessible to them in a way it wasn't made accessible to me?" To make Shakespeare more accessible, Kate tried to move back and forth between the play and her students' experiences, hoping that students would approach the text with new insight after reflecting on their own lives.

In teaching the play, Kate focused on a close reading of the text in class. First she had students read aloud from the play, scene by scene. After discussing the language and general meaning of the passage, Kate led discussions on the text, focusing on the themes of the tension between order and chaos in the play, the search for identity, and the relationship of nature and society. In these discussions, Kate occasionally referred to other Shakespearean plays; for example, in talking about the theme of order or the role of the fool, Kate discussed *King Lear*. In keeping with her desire to have students reflect on their own lives in relation to the play, Kate asked students about their own experiences and ideas. She also asked students to paraphrase passages of the play in contemporary language.

In addition to an in-class writing assignment on a dramatic monologue, Kate assigned a final project, in which students made a 10-minute class presentation on a topic of their choice related to *A Midsummer Night's Dream*; possible presentations included performing and analyzing a scene or passage from the play, discussing historical perspectives on fairies, or relating the play to other works of literature.

Kate characterized her general pedagogical strategy as prodding students into telling her what they found in the text, but said that in this unit, she also began telling them more about what she thought they should be looking for. On the final day of the unit, Kate told the students that although they usually participated in class discussion, on this day she wanted to talk about the play. She then provided an overview of the interrelationship of the themes of chaos and order, and nature and society, emphasizing the structure of the play.

> We start in the court world and from the palace we shift to the artisans. . . . Look at what Shakespeare is doing in setting up the play this way. You could find it in other plays. If you had all read *King Lear*, we could see patterns. . . . If you have read *King Lear*, think of the disorder that begins the play. We start in a lot of disorder. In *Lear*, we start with the civilized world in disorder and then Lear goes into nature and comes back a different man. But that's a tragedy. This is a comedy. Different tones. We start with disorder. The lovers seek refuge in nature, but they find themselves the puppets of nature.

During this lesson, students made a number of analogies between the play and other works they had read, such as *Huck Finn* and *The Odyssey*, and fictional characters from Walt Disney. Kate explored one student's analogy between Puck and Tom Sawyer, but ignored the other students' comments. Generally, Kate asked students questions about the text to initiate a discussion, in which the students eagerly participated.

In talking about how she might teach *A Midsummer Night's Dream* again, Kate suggested that she would want to have more of a plan of the specific things she wanted students to get out of the play, something she had not done this time. In thinking about how to teach the play to a larger class of less able and less motivated students, Kate commented that she would probably not choose to teach in that kind of environment. However, she went on to say that if she found herself in that kind of situation, she would concentrate less on analysis and more on enjoyment. Acknowledging the need to find a way to "hook" students into the play, Kate was not sure what kind of hook she could use that would enable the students to get past the difficulties of Shakespearean language: "I'd want to get a hook. I don't know how I'd teach if I couldn't get them hooked. Well, that's what I don't know [is how to get them hooked]. The whole task is to get through the language, to find out what's underneath the language . . . but you've got to work to get through the language."

Kate's difficulty in rethinking how she might teach the play to a different group of students suggests that while possessing a general sense of the need to get students personally involved with the play, she lacked specific strategies for "hooking" students.

Learning from the Apprenticeship of Observation

Kate acquired much of her pedagogical content knowledge through her apprenticeship of observation as a student in high school and college. Kate's knowledge of student understanding was clearly shaped by her own experiences as a student. In thinking through what made English difficult for students, Kate commented, "I don't know what's difficult for them . . . I'm having a hard time with this question. I don't know yet really. I can think back to what I had difficulty with. Will that help?"

In assessing what materials would be appropriate for her students, Kate also referred to her own experiences. Nowhere is the influence of the apprenticeship of observation more evident than in her knowledge of curriculum. In choosing curriculum materials during the planning interview, Kate reiterated that she thought back to her own high school curriculum in making decisions about which texts to select.

> I should also say that for a lot of these, because I read them in high school, what pops up for me are the ones that I really enjoyed. "Oh, I liked that one, so that would be good." But I have to be careful because I don't want to just choose which I related to, because other students might relate to other ones.

Kate's experiences as a student also shaped her knowledge of instructional strategies, as she used techniques she had observed her own high school teachers and college professors using. In describing a good and a bad teacher, Kate contrasted two of her high school English teachers; the good teacher served as an image of Kate's conception of teaching as a process of stimulating and probing.

> He's the one who really taught me to read a book and I got really excited about literature in the eleventh grade. And I could contrast him to the teacher I had the year before . . . when she was trying to introduce poetry to us . . . I felt she had some stuff she was trying to shove down our throats. And this other man was probing us and throwing things out for us to catch. Now I was one of the ones who caught it and most of the

> class didn't—they were out of it. So he probably wasn't a good teacher in that perspective, but for me he was a wonderful teacher.

Kate also mentioned college courses as sources of instructional strategies. From one professor, she borrowed the idea of reading a small piece of text in great detail.

> I would say as a teacher that [the English courses] influenced me in a sense by helping to qualify me to even teach the subject, by being introduced to the material, and also borrowing different techniques that I learned from the professors . . . the example of [the professor] in the modern period looking at something very closely. So that when I was teaching *The Odyssey*, I could help them to take one small passage and really look at it and see what was going on.

Kate later commented that as this strategy did not work well with her own students, she altered her approach in teaching the next work of literature. "I'm teaching *Huck Finn* very differently from the way I was teaching *The Odyssey*. When I was teaching *The Odyssey*, I looked at it so closely and went into such depth that it was hard sometimes to feel that I was providing the large picture."

Although Kate never put these two comments together, their juxtaposition suggests that the strategies Kate borrowed from her college professor were less successful in her secondary classroom. This situation also illustrates the conflict between what Kate learned from her apprenticeship of observation and her own goals for teaching. While Kate believed in the need to make connections between literature and her students' lives, in classroom discussions of works, she fell back on close textual analysis and analyses of structural features of a text, arguably the dominant strategy in college English courses. When students made analogies between a text and their experiences or other works, Kate sometimes ignored them, explaining that she saw their analogies as attempts to get her off track rather than as windows into their attempts to understand the unfamiliar in terms of the familiar.

Learning from Experience

Kate attributed much of her acquisition of knowledge about teaching to her actual experience in classrooms. Her experiences in Japan teaching English as a second language had given her some understanding of the skills involved in teaching, although she commented that Japanese and American students required distinctly different styles of instruction; while she needed to draw her Japanese students out, she found herself struggling to contain her American students. She also indicated that her directing experiences provided her with a wealth of knowledge about group dynamics, which was readily transferred to classroom management.

Her knowledge of how to teach English, however, or her pedagogical content knowledge, was less directly attributed to her teaching experience. As was suggested earlier, her knowledge about curriculum came primarily from her own experiences as a student, and her conceptions of teaching English resulted less from experience than from her philosophy about theater and general philosophy of teaching. The one area of pedagogical content knowledge she attributed to her teaching experiences was her knowledge of students' understanding of English. Although she found it difficult to predict what students might find difficult or easy or to describe their preconceptions about English, she also reported learning about students' understanding through her exchanges with students in her classroom. On the subject of what students find difficult about the study of poetry she commented, "Back to the question of what difficulties students have. I guess I found out by doing where their difficulties are." Classroom experiences enabled Kate to discover what works were appropriate for her students, and which aspects of literature, grammar, or writing proved problematic.

Perhaps as revealing as what Kate did learn from experience is what she did not learn from classroom experience. While Kate gained a sense of the topics and texts that proved difficult for students, she did not learn more general frameworks regarding the purposes or specific strategies for teaching writing or literature. Kate learned about a different way to think about teaching writing not through experience but through her friend, who shared both a specific book and the more general ideas she gained through participation in an in-service workshop. Experience alone did not teach Kate about developing curricular plans and objectives for her students' learning. In fact, Kate actually seemed to discover the notion of developing specific objectives for her students during the course of one of our interviews, something that will be discussed in the next section. Learning from experience, then, can be haphazard, dependent to a certain extent on chance.

Kate's willingness and desire to learn from other teachers set her apart from Jake and Lance. Despite her eagerness to learn from others, however, the structure of schools allowed her little opportunity to take advantage of the wisdom of more experienced teachers. No formal structure existed in Kate's school, outside of departmental meetings, to provide assistance to beginning teachers. While Kate suggested that she would ask colleagues for advice before teaching an actual course in American literature, for example, she mentioned relatively few instances of actually learning from other teachers.

PLANNING FOR INSTRUCTION: REVIEWING OR RETHINKING?

When Jake, Kate, and Lance talked about preparing to teach Shakespeare, they all mentioned that because they were knowledgeable about Shakespearean drama, they felt little need to plan. In describing how he planned to teach *Romeo and Juliet*, Lance said he re-read the play, marked passages for students to memorize, and looked up the exact names of the sources Shakespeare had used in writing the play. Jake commented that while he had to read *The Merchant of Venice* for the first time before teaching it, he felt confident of his knowledge about Shakespeare and as a result spent little time planning to teach the play. Jake's plans invoked "a general idea of what I want to say." Kate stated that she relied on her knowledge of *A Midsummer Night's Dream* in lieu of specific planning; "I had read the play many times and felt I understood it pretty well, so I was basically trusting my instinct that when things came up, I would know how to respond." None of these teachers received guidelines from their schools about how to plan for instruction.

All three teachers equated subject matter preparation with planning for teaching. Jake commented that because he knew so much more about literature than his students, he had little need to plan; he gave an example of going in to lecture about Shakespeare with only a quarter page of notes. Lance and Kate also trusted their knowledge of the subject matter to guide them in knowing how to structure class discussions. Lance, however, recognized the need to "rethink" *Romeo and Juliet* before teaching it again. How he would rethink the play, however, remained obscure, with Lance reiterating the difficulty of thinking of the play in simpler ways. Kate seemed to discover the very notion of unit planning in the course of one of our interviews, when she talked about how she might teach *A Midsummer Night's Dream* another time.

> If I teach the play again, I'm sure that I would have more of a plan about what specific things I wanted them to get out of the play, because I didn't have that. . . . I'm guessing that in all of my courses, I'll look ahead a lot more. You know, as I say it, this sounds better and better. Actually to think about . . . if there are three things I want them to get out of this, what are they? Write them down and make sure that they get them. Because I certainly have not approached any class like that.

In this comment, Kate began to make the distinction between reviewing the subject matter and planning explicitly for student learning. While it is significant that Kate arrived at this realization about the value of planning, it is equally noteworthy that the comment was made at the end of her first year of teaching and in the context of an interview that specifically asked about her goals for student learning.

KNOWLEDGE, BELIEF, AND TEACHING CONTEXT

Kate began her teaching with different assumptions about the field of English than did the other teachers without formal teacher education. Unlike Jake and Lance, who saw English as revolving around the study of literature, Kate saw communication as the core of English. Her purposes for teaching focused not on the transmission of knowledge but on the transformation of students. These differing beliefs about both the subject matter and teaching, in addition to her prior experiences as both a teacher of English as a Second Language and a director, help account for Kate's ability to make the transition to high school teaching without the degree of frustration expressed by Jake or Lance. Already in possession of a broader vision of English and of teaching, Kate did not have to give up her prior assumptions about teaching.

Yet Kate also taught in a context in which students were eager to learn and able to respond to her probes; there existed "a presumption of shared identity" between teacher and students (Jackson, 1986). Kate saw her students as being like herself, and to a large extent they were, both culturally and intellectually. In this regard, Kate's teaching context offered a close match between her vision of teaching and the abilities and inclinations of her students, a match that seemed less apparent in the contexts in which Lance and Jake taught. Kate implicitly recognized, in her description of her high school English teacher who taught her to enjoy literature, the importance of this match between a teacher's style and students' characteristics: "Now I was one of the ones who caught it and most of the class didn't—they were out of it. . . . But for me he was a wonderful teacher." Kate's vision of teaching as stimulating students by throwing out provocative ideas depends, for its success, on having students who are both able and willing to make the catch.

The experiences of Lance, Jake, and Kate all suggest the ways in which these beginning teachers relied on their subject matter knowledge and apprenticeships of observation during both high school and college in constructing their knowledge and beliefs about teaching English. The differences between Kate and Jake, moreover, illustrate the ways in which specific conceptions of the subject matter, beliefs about teaching, and teaching context contribute to a particular pedagogical understanding of the subject matter. Both Jake's conception of English and his motivation for teaching focused less on the reader/student than on the literary text. Unlike Kate's rather broad vision of English as communication, Jake believed that English centers around the explication of literary texts. He entered teaching in order to communicate his own love and enthusiasm for literature; in contrast to Kate's vision of personal transformation, his conception of teaching features transmission of knowledge. Perhaps Jake would have felt less frustrated in a teaching context more like Kate's, in which he could work with engaged and enthusiastic students. Although he began teaching with "the presumption of shared identity," he quickly discovered that his students were not like him intellectually, a discovery that made teaching more difficult for him and caused him to think about teaching older students, who would be more like himself.

In the next chapter, we will encounter three teachers who, in addition to their subject matter knowledge and apprenticeships of observation, drew upon their professional preparation in their construction of pedagogical content knowledge.

— 3 —

Learning from Professional Education

Steven, Vanessa, and Megan all graduated from the same program of teacher education with masters degrees in education and teaching credentials for secondary English. The program from which they graduated was a fifth-year, graduate level program, emphasizing strong subject-specific preparation in English and a commitment to preparing reflective secondary-school teachers. Students entered the program in the summer, when they took three courses, including a curriculum and instruction course in their subject area, and observed in an on-campus educational summer program. During the remaining three quarters, students taught in local schools, either as interns or as student teachers, for two periods each morning, returning to campus in the afternoon for further coursework. The subject-specific component of the program in English included two quarters of Curriculum and Instruction in English and an elective course, Methods of Teaching Writing, which all three of these graduates took. In addition, students were encouraged to take two elective courses in their subject matter. Other requirements included courses in educational theories, educational psychology, adolescence, the psychology of learning, social science for teachers, and reading in the content areas, in addition to a seminar on issues in secondary-school teaching.

STEVEN: REVISION IN THE CLASSROOM

Steven's case presents the possibility for within-case analysis of the knowledge acquired through teacher education, since he worked as a teaching intern in a private school prior to his professional education. Steven entered teaching because he loved literature and saw teaching as a way to continue his involvement with literature; his initial vision of teaching English recalled his senior seminar in Renaissance literature. Through his teaching experience, Steven discovered that he enjoyed working with students as much as he enjoyed discussing literature, and he entered teacher education to pursue a career in teaching. Through his subject-specific courses, Steven constructed a new vision of what it meant to teach literature in secondary school, a vision that was greatly influenced by the ideas of his professor of English education.

Intellectual Biography

Steven graduated from a prestigious private university with a degree in English. He began his academic career, however, as a biology major, switching to English in his junior year. In the fall of his junior year, he took two very influential English classes, a course in American short fiction, which he identified as his best English class, and a course in Shakespeare. He spent the remainder of his junior year abroad. While in England, he took classes in Shakespeare and Chaucer, an experience that helped the literature to come alive for him. Steven's favorite writers were Shakespeare and early twentieth-century American writers. He felt his strength in English was his ability to "look at various points of view on a particular issue and see the other sides of issues that writers are writing about." Steven found it easy to look at a work as a whole and to identify patterns and themes.

Conceptions of English

Steven believed that English centers around the expression of ideas. While the prototypical forms for expression encompass the different genres of literature, Steven also included less typical forms of expression in his definition of English.

> I feel that English is the expression of ideas, and that we have certain forms that we use and that tend to be real popular—you know, poetry and that kind of stuff—but [English also incorporates] things that people would not automatically assume to be conventional devices, such as editorials and articles and almost anything written.

Steven characterized an expert in English as both well-read and well-rounded.

> Well-read and open-minded would be the two things [that characterize an expert in English] . . . perhaps not necessarily the classics, but well-read in a variety of different types of literature, not just novels, not just

> one time period, and not just the classics, but a wide range of topics, of eras, of authors, genres. Essentially, just as many things as a person can get their hands on . . . but I think that it's real important if you're going to know English, that you know about drama, you know about poetry, and you know about novels and short stories, but that you also know about the different conditions that Dickens wrote in and Faulkner wrote in.

Being open-minded, according to Steven, meant being prepared to consider different ideas and to allow a text to challenge one's prior perceptions.

> The willingness to look at different ideas and ideas that are not your own and to at least consider them. Sometimes that's hard . . . but refusing to look at an issue or an idea from a different point of view is, I think, dangerous. . . . In English, if a person has his or her set of ideas and then takes those ideas and approaches a work and instead of letting the work add on to those ideas, but puts the work into his or her ideas, that can be detrimental to the reader and limiting as far as what the work can do for you.

Steven's conception of English emphasized the expression of ideas—authors' expression of ideas through a broad range of literary forms, as well as readers' expression of their interpretations of that literature. Steven's definition of English, however, was not confined to literature, as he included journalism as well as "anything written."

Entry into Teaching

Steven originally considered a career in teaching during his senior year of college, when he was casting about for a direction. Seeing teaching as a way to extend his literary pursuits, Steven saw his initial motivation for teaching as his own enjoyment of the subject matter.

> When I was a senior, I knew that I really enjoyed English and I really enjoyed discussing ideas and that kind of stuff. And then all of a sudden, it became time to start thinking about a job and the real world. . . . And there were a lot of ideas and opportunities out there that I'd been thinking about pursuing. But becoming a teacher seemed a way for me to continue my enjoyment of the study of literature and ideas. And so initially, that was my purpose and my goal, to be able to continue that for myself and also to pass on my enthusiasm to students.

As Steven had never tutored or taught before, he wanted to find a "low-key" experience to provide an introduction to teaching "just to see what teaching was all about . . . and then if I decided, yeah, I really do like this, then to go into some sort of teacher training." Steven found a job in a small parochial school as an athletic director; in addition to coaching and supervising the sports class, he was to have responsibility for one class. However, when one of the teachers did not show up in the fall, Steven volunteered to take over his classes. Steven found himself teaching two eighth-grade English classes, an eighth-grade U.S. history class, and a seventh-grade math class, all in addition to his coaching responsibilities.

Not surprisingly, Steven found himself overwhelmed by his first teaching experience. The most challenging aspect, he suggested, was trying to figure out what he was supposed to be doing in his classes and how to do it. While he was able to use his textbook in the history class as a guide for structuring the course, he had no idea about what to do in his English classes. He first tried to think back to his own experience in eighth grade, admitting that he was "grabbing at straws."

> It was an incredible transition going from a seminar on Renaissance poetry to an eighth-grade English class. It was about as radical as you can get. And it was not a valuable experience for those kids. . . . I had no idea what to do, and did not receive any real help from the administration or from the department chairs or from other teachers. I just didn't know what I was doing or how to go about it. I was given the books and told, "O.K., go in there and teach," but I really didn't have any idea. And I tried to think back on how my eighth-grade teacher taught, and did a pretty bad job of that. . . . The history was a lot easier because I had a textbook. And so at least I had a lesson plan. And I could say, "O.K., go answer the questions." That may not be a very effective way of teaching history, but at least it was something. I was grabbing at straws in the English class.

In retrospect, Steven identified his major problem as his lack of overall goals for his students; "really not having any objectives when I went into the classroom, having activities but not objectives that first year really was a problem both for me and for the students." The ill-defined nature of the English curriculum left him unsure of what to do or why. Without a clear conception of what he was supposed to accomplish, Steven floundered in the classroom.

Believing that many of his problems stemmed from the fact that he was not really able to teach literature to his eighth graders, Steven jumped at the chance to swap classes with another teacher during the second semester; he exchanged his eighth graders for junior and senior English classes. He discovered, however, that his ideas about teaching literature did not work with the juniors and seniors either.

> So then, the second semester I was teaching juniors and seniors in literature. And that was also a fiasco. They weren't eighth graders, but then I was suddenly teaching literature, as I had thought I wanted to do, but I didn't realize that these are high school students and all that kind of stuff and started teaching it as if it were a college class, expecting students should just be able to talk about the work and want to do that and just have discussions all period long and it would be real valuable. That isn't the case. Students just don't burst out and want to talk about a work. And so that was really a shock. Trying to force it on the kids was clearly a mistake and not really knowing what else to do . . . isn't that what you do in an English class is talk about literature and ideas?

Despite this disastrous beginning, Steven discovered that he really did enjoy teaching, but not for the reason he had expected. While he had decided to teach due to his love of literature, he found that what he really enjoyed in the classroom were not the literary discussions but the interactions with students.

> What I found was that it wasn't the literature that was really so appealing. What I found was that it was the kids themselves, and working with them, that made it enjoyable and made me want to be there. . . . So that was pretty much the reason why I decided to go into [the teacher education program].

Steven applied and was accepted to the teacher education program at his alma mater, an experience that dramatically altered his ideas about teaching English.

Conceptions of Teaching English

Steven's motivation for teaching was not the only element that underwent a major transformation during his first experience with teaching and his professional preparation. Steven reported that his ideas about teaching English changed drastically as a result of his curriculum and instruction courses at the university. Prior to his professional preparation, Steven believed that literature was at the center of the high school English curriculum. During teacher education, he came to believe that student expression of ideas through writing was the major focus of secondary-school English.

> Again, it changed from my original idea. I was really excited about literature and that kind of stuff and when I got to the classroom and started working with students, what became most important was their writing and their expression of their ideas, and to come up with their ideas. And the best way to come up with their ideas, I found, was through the pen and to write them out. So my job as an English teacher is to teach students to express themselves better.

Steven attributed this change in focus from literature to writing to his professor of English education. Not only did his participation in his curriculum and instruction classes change the focus of Steven's ideas about the English curriculum, it also changed his ideas about the way to teach writing. When he entered teacher education, Steven believed that teaching writing involved teaching students about grammar and sentence diagramming. His subject-specific courses, however, introduced him to a new way of thinking about teaching writing.

> I think it was [the professor of English education] and his approach that sort of shook me. I had a long way to go to get from where I started to get to this point. So I started there, and I remember the first day of Professor X's course. I was saying, "Well, sure, you know, kids need to diagram sentences." It wasn't until I had read some studies and done some more reading on it that I found that, jeez, in fact it's not very valuable at all. It seems we don't see the connection between diagramming a sentence and writing one that makes sense.

Steven came to believe that to teach writing, a teacher must first focus on the content of a piece before worrying about form or correctness, suggesting that students get discouraged if teachers focus too much on errors in their writing. "I think we need to stress more of what do you want to say. And when we force the form on them so quickly and so rigidly that unless they have an innate sense of what good writing is and what their ideas are, they're going to be real hung up on expressing themselves." Steven believed that instead of concentrating on correct grammar and form, teachers need to get students involved and comfortable with writing by having them write about issues they care about deeply. Once students are engaged with the piece, Steven believed they would be more willing to work to improve the form and grammar of their writing. This framework for thinking about teaching writing also stresses the need for teachers to pay attention to the different processes involved in writing, rather than simply grading the product. Steven reported having his students first brainstorm ideas or engage in "pre-writing" exercises and later work in "peer response groups" to revise their work.

Although Steven began to see writing as the core of the English curriculum, he still believed in the value of teaching literature. His ideas of how to engage students in discussions of literature, however, changed from his initial teaching experience. While Steven reported running his first English classes like "a college seminar on Renaissance literature" in which students were expected to find the literature intrinsically interesting, he came to believe that it was his job as a teacher to build bridges between the literature and students' lives.

> Usually the way I teach literature is I try to have the students relate to the work, and that's usually my philosophy. I think in college and perhaps in A.P. classes that the students there are motivated and have really good skills in reading, writing, and thinking, that they tend to be able to make the connections there, but in most of the regular classes, I think it's my job to make the connection between the work and their lives. As an adult who's seen part of this world I can relate to this piece, but to get the students, who are forced to be in my classroom and forced to read this, my job is to make them interested in the work as well, and to see some significance to their own lives. So what I would do is try to think of a bridge between this piece and their lives.

Steven preferred to teach literature within thematic units, in which the literature is organized around a specific theme, usually one that connects with student experience. Steven attributed his new understanding of the need to relate literature to personal experience and the use of thematic units to his curriculum and instruction courses.

Teaching Context

On completion of his professional preparation, Steven accepted a job at a multi-racial, suburban high school. He taught four sections of senior accelerated English and a section of freshman English during his first semester. The senior class to which he taught *Hamlet* included approximately 23 students. Steven commented that the accelerated label was somewhat of a misnomer, as it was the middle of three tracks at the senior level, standing between advanced placement and special help courses. Steven reported that the accelerated classes incorporated students with a wide range of skill levels.

Teaching *Hamlet*, Round Two

Steven actually taught *Hamlet* twice, once while he was a teaching intern during teacher education and again during his first year of full-time teaching. For his first attempt, Steven adopted what he termed a "scholarly" approach toward teaching the play. He believed that students needed to understand the play word for word, an approach he felt ultimately left the students bored and uninterested.

> What I tried to do last year . . . was sort of a scholarly approach to the whole thing, and the kids just didn't care. Last year I figured that they needed to know every, I mean *every*, single word. . . . And they just weren't into it and couldn't understand it and it was sort of force-fed and I don't think they got a whole lot out of it.

For his second attempt, Steven decided to use a very different approach to teaching the play. He focused less on the language and form and more on the issues addressed in the play that students could connect with their own lives.

> And my intention wasn't really to read *Hamlet*; instead, it was to show it, this drama, and if the students could pick up on what was happening and the issues involved, then I would consider it to be a success . . . so it wasn't "here's a passage and translate it," it was more, "what's going on essentially in the bigger picture."

Steven's major concern was how to help students connect with the play. Because students were unlikely to make this connection with Shakespeare on their own, he believed his job as a teacher involved constructing bridges between the play and their lives.

> I want them to be able to see a connection and to be interested in [the play]. I taught it last year too and I didn't do this . . . I was more concerned with them understanding the language, and it really didn't work. . . . My students aren't going to make that connection on their own, so that I've got to provide the bridge for them. And so that's why we're going to take this approach.

The approach Steven chose was to provide an elaborate introduction to the play, without mentioning it by name. He first tried to think about which issues raised in the play would be most relevant to his students' lives. Although Steven identified a number of potential issues, he decided to focus on one that seemed particularly relevant: "And what I tried to do was come up with sort of a destruction of the nuclear family as essentially what happens in *Hamlet* and to get their reaction to it."

Steven reported that the topic of separation and divorce provoked very lively and intense class discussions, with a high level of student participation. Steven commented that these discussions began to "hook" the students into the play. "And so listening to their ideas and talking about what they would do in that particular situation and what they'd do in their real lives, I began to sort of get them hooked a little bit."

Having decided not to require students to read the play, Steven planned to show them the videotape. Due to logistical problems with the length of classes and the availability of the video recorder, Steven ended up not being able to show his students the whole play, but instead mixed and matched scenes. Prior to the viewing, Steven provided the students with summaries of each act, which they read before watching the act. In discussions of the videotape, he tried to move back and forth between the play and their own experiences. In retrospect, however, Steven felt that students spent too much time talking about their own experiences and too little time talking about *Hamlet*; "the problem was that people tended to talk pretty much about their own experiences and leave Hamlet aside." This became Steven's major frustration with his second approach toward teaching *Hamlet*.

> And what was hard was I didn't want to beat a dead horse, but I wanted to maintain the enthusiasm. . . . I think the problem that I had, driving home at night, was wondering whether I was getting enough out of *Hamlet* itself as a work, or was I just kind of doing lip service to it and really focusing on something else. I don't know.

By focusing on questions of divorce and murder, Steven felt he kept the interest level of the class incredibly high, mentioning that during this time he had almost no problems with classroom management. He also believed that the focus on student experiences tended to obscure the play itself, pushing *Hamlet* into the background of the unit. While in his internship he felt he focused too much on textual analysis, in this unit he believed there was too little discussion of the text. In teaching the play again, Steven said he would like to move toward middle ground.

For the final exam, Steven asked the students to do an essay in which they chose a characteristic of Hamlet's and demonstrated how that characteristic exists in people today: "I wanted to see evidence from the play that would show Hamlet was motivated or whatever." The class spent a week working on the paper in class, first coming up with quotations to support their choice of characteristics and then working in groups to develop their ideas. Steven reported that on each day the class worked on one element or part of the paper. The students completed their final drafts at home. Steven was somewhat disappointed with the final papers: "[They] didn't really stand out as being really personal and really alive, with voice." Instead, he felt students approached the assignment as one more thing to do for school.

In discussing how he might teach *Hamlet* to different levels of classes, Steven suggested that in teaching the play to an advanced placement level class, he would be more likely to emphasize analysis of the play.

> I would definitely try to merge [the two approaches] a little bit more than I did, that instead of what happens, why does it happen and to up the ante a little bit . . . and to try to analyze it a little bit, rather than just to say, this is what he does here, that's what he does and sort of give lip service to the whys.

In teaching the play to a lower-level class, Steven would emphasize personal experiences and put less emphasis on an understanding of the play itself.

The Influence of Subject-Specific Coursework

Steven presents the possibility for within-case analysis, as he taught both before and after he received professional preparation. While we have to rely on self-report data to get a sense of Steven's approach to teaching prior to teacher education, by his account he closely resembled Jake and Lance. Like both Jake and Lance, he decided to teach on the basis of his love for literature and considered literature to be at the center of the English curriculum. Expecting to run his classes like the college seminars from which he had recently graduated, Steven found, to his surprise, that high school students were not as eager to engage in literary discussions as were college English majors. The central problem he reportedly encountered, however, was the lack of a framework to guide his decisions about what to do in his English classes. Without even a textbook as a crutch, Steven limped along in his eighth-grade English classes, unsure of where or how to proceed. Like Jake, he thought back to his own eighth-grade English teacher, hoping for enlightenment through memory. He recognized, however, that memory was a poor guide.

His eagerness to teach the upper-level courses in which he could teach literature is again reminiscent of Jake and Lance, who both talked about their preference for older students with whom they could discuss literature in depth. Steven discovered that the approach he was used to from college did not work with juniors or seniors, but he did not seem able to develop an alternative approach on his own. Only through teacher education did he develop, in his terms, a radically different notion of what it meant to teach English.

Steven's experience suggests that the lessons presented through professional preparation are not acquired just as easily through practical experience. In fact, in hindsight, Steven attributed learning almost nothing from his early experience in the classroom. He discovered that he enjoyed the interaction with students enough to pursue professional preparation. He also learned that his unexamined conceptions about teaching English did not seem to work in the classroom, which may have made him more receptive to the approach suggested by his professor of English education. Steven's comments, however, do not suggest that without the intervention of teacher education he would have arrived at the conception of teaching English to which he became committed.

Steven's experience in his curriculum and instruction courses seemed to have drastically altered his ideas about teaching English. As he commented, he had a long way to go to get from his original notions to the ideas presented in his courses. He came to professional preparation believing that teaching writing was a matter of teaching grammar, and that teaching literature involved teaching students the techniques he had used as an English major. From this perspective, the ideas of his curriculum and instruction course struck him as being radical.

> The ideas [of the English C & I course] seemed so radical to me after teaching . . . for a year and doing the sentence diagramming and that's the way you teach writing. So you come out of this completely backwards notion from that, and then to come around and believe it was surprising. . . . It just changed the whole way I looked at the teaching of writing and also writing itself.

According to Steven, the foundation on which his curriculum and instruction courses rested was the concept of instructional scaffolding, which Steven understood as the belief that students need support as they learn to do things on their own, and that it is the teacher's role to provide the support, or scaffolding, for the students.

> [All three courses] essentially revolved around the same theme. They just had variations on that theme, on [how to] make the work accessible to your students. Don't demand that they write flawless essays the first draft and turn them in. Don't assign something and just collect it once and give them a grade, turn it back and move on to the next assignment, that there has to be some process. . . . Again a variation on the theme of support your students and the idea of scaffolding . . . that you have to support students and you can't just throw out the idea, that you have to give them something to work with when they move on to their own assignments . . . and so that idea is pretty much the basis for all three of the classes.

This concept of scaffolding, and the accompanying notion of student ownership, encompasses what Steven learned about teaching writing as a process and about teaching literature through connection to student experience. These ideas affected how he responded to other professional coursework; he related most strongly to the theories presented in his philosophical foundations course that he believed "tied in rather nicely" with the ideas he was encountering in his curriculum and instruction course. These ideas also became the cornerstone of his internship experience, which he described as an attempt to put this new philosophy into action.

> I was an intern for two classes both semesters. Out of that, I think a lot of it was after developing theories during the summer and changing philosophies, putting them into action and having it work to an extent . . . not all the time, clearly, but for the most part to have success.

Steven's description of his two approaches to teaching *Hamlet* captures the nature of the transformation of his ideas. His first approach mirrored the general approach he took prior to teacher education, in which he attempted to teach *Hamlet* on the level at which he understood the play himself. Using what he termed "a scholarly approach," Steven required students to do close critical analyses of the text, examining the play word for word. His second approach, taken during his first year of full-time teaching, reflected, and even overgeneralized, the lessons of his subject-specific teacher education coursework, as he tried to construct a bridge between students' experiences and Shakespeare. The final paper for the unit incorporated the various stages of the writing process about which Steven had learned, from prewriting activities, through revision and editing. Yet in his second version of *Hamlet* in the classroom, Steven did not ask his students to read the play at all; instead they watched most of it on videotape. While consistent with his own understanding of a new approach toward teaching English, Steven's decision to have students watch, rather than read, Shakespeare may represent an instance of overgeneralizing from teacher education.

Overgeneralizing the Lessons of Teacher Education

Steven's dramatic conversion to a new way of thinking about teaching English swung him to the other extreme of a continuum. While he first believed in the value of close textual analysis, he then appeared to discard the text altogether. Steven's experience suggests that beginning teachers may go to extremes as they learn to rethink their purposes for and approaches to teaching particular subject matter. In fact, the overgeneralization of new perspectives may represent a necessary stage in the construction of new knowledge (Ammon, 1988; Stoddard, 1988). Steven's reflection on his second treatment of *Hamlet* indicates that he recognized that he may have swung too far away from the text in his second approach; still dissatisfied, he planned to integrate the two approaches when he taught the play again.

VANESSA: FROM JOURNALISM TO TEACHING

Vanessa entered her professional preparation with less subject matter background than any of the other teachers in this study. As a journalism major, Vanessa took fewer literature courses than the English and comparative literature majors. She found it difficult to separate her ideas about English as a discipline from her ideas about teaching English as a school subject. In fact, much of what Vanessa reported learning about literature she claimed to have acquired during her year of teacher education. Vanessa's ideas about the teaching of both writing and literature were shaped by the curriculum and instruction courses taught by her professor of English education.

Intellectual Biography

Vanessa entered a large private college with the intention of becoming an English major, as reading was her favorite activity. She discovered, however, that she disliked the way the English department at her college was organized and the way in which courses were taught. Rethinking her academic plans, Vanessa decided to major in journalism instead of English, since she had always loved writing: "The part of English that I liked the best was writing anyhow. I loved to read, but I liked to do the writing." In the school of public communications, Vanessa took numerous writing courses, specializing in magazine writing.

While she enjoyed her journalism courses, she felt less well prepared in literature than were traditional English majors. As she explained,

> I'm sort of different from a lot of people in that I have less of an English background. . . . I've read millions of different types of books, but I'm not one of those people that's read a whole area of literature, or all these types of authors, or you know, everything by Faulkner; that type of thing is really sketchy. So maybe I've read maybe one book by this author, but I don't really know his background and the information behind it, or his place in the whole scheme of English as much as I feel like I should either.

Vanessa explained, for example, that she never took a Shakespeare course in college. She believed her strengths lay in writing and verbal skills; the area of literature in which she felt most secure was women authors. When Vanessa entered her teacher education program, she elected to take two literature courses—a course on Shakespeare and a course in American short fiction—to strengthen her knowledge of literature. Vanessa felt least secure in the area of grammar, which she did not remember studying formally. "I know the correct way to do a lot of things, but I can't tell you why. And I know how to write sentences correctly, but to tell you what a gerund is . . . I'm really learning it as I go along."

Conceptions of English

Vanessa's conceptions of English as a discipline are not easily separated from her conceptions about teaching English. In reply to a question about the different areas that make up English as a discipline, she included reading, writing, and speaking, the same three areas she used to describe her conception of the high school English curriculum. When asked how the three areas were related within the field of English, she again replied in terms of teaching; she could not teach reading and writing separately, she suggested. As Vanessa exclaimed, "I can't talk about it [English] without talking about teaching." She commented that when taking an American fiction course during her year of teacher education, she did not enjoy "getting down to these really obscure, obscure things" and asked her teaching assistant if she could do lesson plans instead of critical analyses of the literature.

Vanessa believed that an expert in English should "know everything I don't know." She argued that an expert would "really just have to be incredibly well-read"; in addition, an expert would need to be able to write well, speak well, and know grammar well.

Entry into Teaching

Although Vanessa had considered the idea of a teaching career ever since high school, she did not pursue it immediately after college. She suggested that when she graduated, very few people were actually getting teaching jobs. Despite her journalism major, Vanessa decided against a career in this field because she did not like the competitive nature of the profession. She also considered being a librarian, "because books were my favorite thing in the world, so I figured if I can be around books the whole time, then that would be wonderful." In casting about for a direction, she consulted the Yellow Pages, which eventually led her back to the idea of teaching.

> In college I switched to journalism because the part of English I decided I liked best was the writing. But I didn't really like journalism. I didn't like the profession. I didn't like the cut-throat type of thing . . . so here I'd switched from being an English major to a journalism major and really had no idea what I wanted to do. . . . And so I decided well, what do I like to do best in the world? Read. So I looked under "read" in the Yellow Pages and it said "reading centers." So I said, O.K., fine, and I wrote down the names of a couple of reading centers. And I went to the first one and I got hired.

Vanessa worked at this reading center for a year, engaged with a wide variety of students. She subsequently worked as a teacher's aide in reading classes at a local middle school for two more years and served as director of student activities. During these experiences, she discovered that she loved working with students and decided to apply to the teacher education program at the private university nearby.

Vanessa's motivation for teaching stemmed from a number of factors, including her love of reading, her enjoyment of working with kids, and the example of her mother, who was also an English teacher. She insisted, however, that her love of English was not her primary motivation for teaching.

> [I went into teaching] because of teaching, not because of English. . . . A lot of people that I saw went into teaching because they loved English or they loved biology or they loved chemistry. And in my mind, I don't think that's the right reason. I think they should be combined . . . but I think the teaching part of it should take precedence over the subject matter part of it. Because it doesn't matter how qualified you are subject matter wise, if you can't teach and you can't learn to do that, then it doesn't work. Whereas you can, I think, build up all the knowledge that you need to go with the teaching.

Despite this qualification, Vanessa never considered teaching a subject other than English, although she did think about pursuing a double credential in English and history. During her teacher education program, Vanessa taught two English courses at a local public school. As an intern, she had complete responsibility for her courses, but she felt that the other teachers in her department were very helpful and supportive. During her internship, Vanessa participated in an in-service program at the school featuring the Bay Area Writing Project, an experience she found very valuable.

Teaching Context

After completing her credential in English, Vanessa began teaching at a local private college-preparatory school, the same school at which Jake taught. The all-boys school was run by a religious order. During her first year of full-time teaching, Vanessa taught three different English courses: seventh-grade, tenth-grade, and eleventh-grade English. Although the school's purpose was to prepare students for college, the ability of students ranged widely. When she discovered that a number of her tenth graders were limited English speaking, Vanessa spent much of her free time after school tutoring them.

Conceptions of Teaching English

Vanessa felt that the necessity for studying English was self-explanatory; English was the key to everything else.

> You don't have to study anything else, but you have to study English. Because you can't talk, write, know anything unless you study English. It's the key to everything. Of course, that's what I tell my kids. "I know that you have a lot of subjects, but you have really got to do your English homework. It is the most important."

Although Vanessa felt that her goals for students would differ by grade level, her one goal for all her students was to get them to enjoy some aspect of English: "I think a universal [goal] is some enjoyment from the course. . . . I mean, because I love it so much, I just can't imagine them not liking it." In addition to enjoyment, Vanessa wanted her courses to help open doors for students and to enable them to express themselves better, in both writing and speaking.

Vanessa divided the English curriculum into reading, writing, and speaking, and she addressed each one of these parts separately in her comments. In reading, she believed that the literature should be closely connected to student experience. She approved of the curriculum at her school, which included books about "things that are about growing up and things that are about kids." Vanessa believed that an English curriculum should emphasize writing of many different types, since writing helps connect the curriculum to student experience.

> When we do poetry, they write poetry, so that they're always constantly experiencing what it is they're doing, which goes along on the same thing. If it's so far away from their experience of what they are dealing with, then it's so hard for them to like it or do anything with it.

Finally, Vanessa believed students need to speak in class, learning to express and defend their ideas and to become more articulate.

In discussing the difficulties students encounter in English, Vanessa commented that students have problems with reading, talking in front of class, writing, and spelling. From her experience working with remedial students, Vanessa believed that most of these problems stem from a lack of self-confidence. By beginning with easier assignments and literature, Vanessa believed students could develop the confidence with writing and literature that would enable them to tackle more difficult topics. In structuring her curricula, Vanessa always moved from the least difficult texts and topics to the most difficult: "I'm a firm believer in doing it from the easiest to the hardest." Vanessa explained this philosophy in talking about how she might structure a ninth-grade curriculum.

> I mean 90 percent of the kids like *To Kill a Mockingbird* or *Of Mice and Men*. But things they have difficulty with, it's hard for them to accept it, and if they've already not accepted it, then it's really hard to get anything done with it . . . so poetry I usually do closer to the end, where they can feel more comfortable with it. Because I like them to do a lot of writing of poetry and that's kind of a hard thing to do is share their poetry. That's why more of this serious stuff I leave until the end and have them do limericks . . . at the beginning. And then all of a sudden they find themselves writing longer things and better things and it doesn't hurt that much.

Vanessa's belief that students need to begin where they feel most comfortable and then, with the help of a teacher, move on to more challenging topics and activities, guided almost all of her curricular planning.

Teaching *Twelfth Night*

Vanessa taught *Twelfth Night* to her tenth-grade class as part of the school's required curriculum. She had never read the play before and would have preferred to teach *A Midsummer Night's Dream*, which she had both read and seen numerous times. Her class consisted of 22 students, the largest class in the school. Vanessa indicated that when she started teaching this class, she had tremendous discipline problems; by the time she taught the play, however, the class had settled down. Vanessa worried about teaching Shakespeare to these students, many of whom knew English only as a second language. As the class also encompassed a wide range of ability levels, Vanessa thought about using a projects-oriented approach to teaching *Twelfth Night*, an approach advocated by her English supervisor during teacher education and that she had first used in teaching *Romeo and Juliet* to ninth graders during her internship. Vanessa acknowledged the influence of her English supervisor from the university; "I think basically we made it up, but having Mr. X for a supervisor makes you very project oriented."

In organizing her unit on *Twelfth Night*, Vanessa developed lists of three types of projects: writing projects, worth between 50 and 100 points; art projects, worth from 25 to 30 points; and acting projects. Examples of writing projects included rewriting a scene from the play in contemporary English, rewriting the ending of the play, writing diary entries for different characters, or writing a research project on some aspect of the play, such as Shakespearean theater or Elizabethan life. Examples of art projects included illustrating a quotation from the play to show its meaning, illustrating a scene, or making a collage of a character to show what the character was like. Vanessa required each student to do at least a writing project and an art project and to complete enough projects to earn 225 points. One of the reasons Vanessa gave for choosing a projects-oriented approach was the diversity of ability levels in the class.

> The abilities range so much, which is another reason why I like to do the projects, because that way you can have a kid do something on their own level . . . they can still produce what they can produce and they can produce their best, without pulling one kid down or making it be too much of an effort for some of the poorer kids.

In addition to the projects, students were required to paraphrase one page of the play each week. Vanessa also quizzed the students on each act of the play.

Vanessa spent about a month on the play. She began the unit by inviting another teacher at the school, a self-described "Shakespeare freak," to provide an introduction to Shakespeare and Shakespearean theater. She also showed an episode from the television show "Moonlighting" in which the characters acted out *The Taming of the Shrew*. Vanessa felt that showing the television episode helped students to overcome the barrier of Shakespearean language.

> I like "Moonlighting" anyhow, but this sort of helped the kids relate more to the language, because they did *Taming of the Shrew* in the "Moonlighting" episode and they sort of did one-half in Shakespearean language and one-half sort of the special jargon they use, and it was really just fun, and they got an idea that maybe it wasn't so threatening and that's the thing I find the most is that Shakespeare is so threatening

> to some kids. Then when they look at it, they say, "I don't understand it and there's no way I'm going to understand it," and unless you do something that they realize they're having fun and they enjoy it. And I think that 90 percent of the kids ended up enjoying it.

Vanessa's goals for teaching *Twelfth Night* revolved around her desire for students to overcome their fear of Shakespeare.

> To eliminate the fear of Shakespeare I think was the number one goal. Because I think that is one of the worst things. Once they're turned off from it, then they're turned off for good. And I think it's really difficult for the average high school student to really love Shakespeare. And I didn't like him and I was an "A" student . . . and plus for them to sort of unlock and figure out how to read it.

Vanessa also wanted her students to understand the themes of love, deception, and disguise in the play and to see how these themes transcend time.

In describing a typical week in the unit on *Twelfth Night*, Vanessa reported that she usually spent one day a week going over the students' paraphrases of the play; each student explained what his or her page meant and what the characters were saying. On another day the students read the play aloud. A third day was devoted to class discussions, in which the class talked about love, deception and disguise, characterization, and the role of the clown, among other topics. Typically, Vanessa allotted one day a week for students to work on their projects during class time. The final day was spent doing vocabulary drill in preparation for college achievement tests.

Vanessa included two questions about *Twelfth Night* on her final exam for the class. One question asked students to explain how and why deception and disguise are used in the play. The second question provided students with a quotation from the play, which they were to relate to the characters of Malvolio, Orsino, and Olivia.

In teaching the play again, Vanessa said she would like to show a movie of the play or to use a good audio recording. When teaching *Romeo and Juliet*, she showed the first half hour of the movie to introduce her students to the characters and to interest them in the plot, a technique she would like to use again. The next time she taught the play, Vanessa would also require students to do an acting project and would provide clearer guidelines for the research papers. In thinking about teaching the play to a stronger group of students, Vanessa thought she would do more with the characters and themes of the play and require students to write more critical papers about the play, perhaps as many as one three-page paper a week.

Learning Content Through Teaching and Teacher Education

Vanessa's ideas about teaching English were inseparable from her conceptions of English as a discipline. As she commented, "it's really hard to disengage the teaching part of it from the English." She defined the field of English pedagogically, dividing it into "reading, writing, and speaking" and analyzing the relationships among the three areas in terms of how they are taught. For Vanessa, English was what she taught her students.

Part of Vanessa's difficulty in disentangling the discipline of English and English as a secondary-school subject can be traced to her undergraduate background in journalism. With only one exception, she did not believe that her undergraduate English courses influenced her conceptions of English; the one exception was a freshman seminar for English majors. In fact, her notions of English seemed shaped more by her professional preparation than by her undergraduate experience. In ranking the experiences and courses that contributed to her knowledge and beliefs about English, she attributed most of her knowledge about literature to her teaching internship; she needed to learn more about the literature in order to teach it, she argued. In second place, Vanessa ranked a Shakespeare course she took as an elective during teacher education. In third place, Vanessa listed her curriculum and instruction courses and methods of teaching writing course as influences on her conceptions of English. She felt these courses helped her clarify her own ideas and beliefs about English. Part of the process of clarification occurred through interactions with her peers.

> It was just strange how people had their own set ideas of what English was and what you should do with it . . . but it also made you think, when you had these kinds of discussions, you thought about it a lot. "Now do I really believe that?" And it made you question your beliefs, so that's good.

Unlike the other teachers in this study, Vanessa did not enter professional preparation with explicit conceptions of the nature of the subject matter. As she learned about teaching English, she also learned about the field itself. Her concerns about teaching, however, acted as a filter for the knowledge she acquired about English. In a course in American short fiction, for example, she complained that her teaching assistant insisted on talking only about "obscure, obscure" details of the text, while she was interested only in writing lesson plans. "I wanted to do it how it would relate to high school students, and he wanted to do it how it would relate to graduate school, to someone in graduate school in comparative literature." Seeing little value for her teaching in the close textual analysis modeled by her teaching assistant, she placed the literature in the context of teaching, as she wondered how to teach the texts to her students. Vanessa's case suggests that when prospective teachers acquire subject matter knowledge simultaneously with pedagogical content knowledge, a common occurrence in four-year programs of teacher education, pedagogical concerns shape the acquisition of disciplinary knowledge.

Tracing the Influence of Teacher Education

Despite her experiences as a tutor and teacher's aide, Vanessa attributed much of her knowledge about teaching English to her professional preparation. She attributed most of her conceptions about and goals for teaching English to her subject-specific teacher education courses: Curriculum and Instruction in English, Curriculum and Instruction in Literature, and Methods of Teaching Writing. She argued that these courses combined the practical and theoretical, by both giving practical ideas for what to do in classes and encouraging the prospective teachers to think about their reasons for pedagogical decisions.

> Well, [the curriculum and instruction course] was practical, and just thinking about why you're doing it. That's one of the things that [the professor] did the most . . . and this is one of the reasons why I wanted to do this [research] with you and continue to do that, because you stop thinking about why you're doing something, and you just say, "I have to teach this next so this is how I'm going to do it." And it made us think about why we were teaching English and what we wanted them to get out of it, and the goals, all the things that we thought were important . . . that really kept you thinking about it.

In provoking her to think about her goals for teaching English, Vanessa's curriculum and instruction courses enabled her to articulate her purposes for teaching and to connect her purposes with her choice of activities. When asked how she might teach a particular poem, Vanessa indicated her need to think first about her larger goals. "When I teach poetry, I do it with a certain thing in mind. For example, am I teaching them this poem for reasons of showing them a certain form, or am I teaching them a certain theme, or am I connecting a series of poems by a particular poet?"

Vanessa also acknowledged learning a number of instructional strategies through her subject-specific teacher education courses. Her use of a projects-oriented approach to teaching Shakespeare was encouraged by her university supervisor, and many of her ideas about teaching writing came directly from her coursework and the textbooks used in the subject-specific courses. Her knowledge of instructional strategies also developed as a result of her internship experience, in which she first grappled with the complexities of presenting material to students. Many of the ideas Vanessa implemented during her first year of teaching, in fact, evolved from strategies she had tried during her internship.

Like the majority of teachers (Lortie, 1975), Vanessa found her internship experience to be the most valuable aspect of professional preparation. Her experience in the classroom enabled her to test her ideas against the realities of the classroom and the culture of the school.

> There's no better way of teaching than going into the classroom and doing it. . . . I learned just that you can know something and not be able to teach it, so you really have to think about how is the best way to teach this. I learned how to structure the amount of time I was going to do something. I learned what activities would work and what activities wouldn't work. I learned how to make things that they might find boring to be more fun. I learned what things I considered important to teach and what things the school considered important to teach, how to plan my time—everything. How to sort of evaluate myself as a teacher.

Most of what Vanessa claimed to have learned from her internship involves the practicalities of teaching and knowledge of student understanding—pacing oneself, assessing the feasibility of activities, planning one's time, capturing student interest. Supervised teaching allowed Vanessa to develop and refine the skills she would need in the classroom; it did not necessarily provide her with a blueprint for what she should accomplish. This hypothesis is supported by the fact that across all areas of pedagogical content knowledge, Vanessa said she learned most about curricular materials and the English curriculum through her internship. Again, her actual experience in schools taught her which books were usually taught in the ninth-grade curriculum, which books were appropriate for juniors, and which books were available for the teaching of writing. Her teacher education coursework, however, provided her with the ideas about teaching writing that enabled her to critique the texts in terms of their adherence to a particular model of teaching writing. Her contact with students in the field also taught Vanessa to assess beforehand what things might prove difficult for students.

Vanessa's acquisition of knowledge during teacher education follows a pattern similar to that of her colleagues in this study. Reportedly developing her conceptions of the purposes of teaching English and a theoretical understanding of the English curriculum through her subject-specific coursework, Vanessa also acquired a repertoire of instructional strategies, through both coursework and fieldwork, with which to implement her vision of teaching English. Her experience in schools provided her with knowledge of student understanding of English and knowledge of the English curriculum as it existed in specific schools.

Vanessa also acquired a belief in the importance of collegial interaction. She felt strongly that much of her learning occurred through her interactions with peers during her teacher education program, in which sharing and collegiality were encouraged. Much of her knowledge of instructional strategies came from the sharing of lesson plans and ideas that occurred during meetings of the prospective English teachers.

> The English group that we had was so helpful. And I know this is something that we all miss the most, is having people there for the feedback. And we would do things all the time where we would share . . . our stuff . . . and we would xerox off a unit that worked really well, or a day that worked well, or a specific lesson that worked really well and then xerox it off and bring it in and we would explain and exchange. And that was one of the most helpful things. And we still do that. I'll call Megan up and I'll say, "Now what did you do with *Catcher in the Rye*?" And I have all my practicum plans in there that people have exchanged and I look them up . . . in fact I'm doing something that Megan did last year, in my class.

As Vanessa indicated, the graduates of this program kept in touch with each other after graduation and continued to share ideas and specific lesson plans.

MEGAN: OPENING THE DOOR FOR LEARNING

During college, Megan studied comparative literature and was actively involved with drama. Her desire to teach reflected both her sense of social responsibility and her past experiences working with children. While Megan entered teaching with a clear understanding of the disciplinary structures of English, she distinguished between knowledge that is essential for the discipline and knowledge that is appropriate for secondary school. Through her professional preparation, Megan acquired both a framework and a language to guide her conceptions of teaching English.

Intellectual Biography

Megan graduated from an elite public university with a degree in comparative literature. As her department required its students to specialize in both a major language and literature and a minor language and literature, Megan chose to study Hebrew as her primary specialization and elected

English as her minor area. In addition to Hebrew literature and language courses and a series of world literature courses, Megan also took a number of survey courses in the English department. As a result of her comparative literature major, Megan felt better versed in world literature than many English majors, but also acknowledged that there were a number of American and British classics that she had not read. For her senior thesis, Megan wrote a comparative analysis of an Israeli and an American author.

In addition to her training in literature, Megan studied drama both at an acting school during high school and during college. At one point, Megan considered a career in theater. Megan also lived in Israel both during and after college. On her first visit, she studied at a university, while on her second visit she worked with new immigrants to the country.

Conceptions of English

Megan believed that the discipline of English comprised two major areas, language and literature. Under language, she included communication, both written and verbal, linguistics, grammar, and speech. The area of literature incorporated both a familiarity with literature and an ability to read critically. Megan felt that in order to study English, one needed to be able to see patterns in a literary work and to be able to find connections. In her own analysis of a poem, Megan paid close attention to the words. Her emphasis on close critical reading of a text allied her most closely with the tradition of New Criticism, in which the text is analyzed through careful attention to the work itself, with no reference to authorial intention or biographical information.

Entry into Teaching

Megan did not seriously consider a career in teaching until after her senior year in college, when she was living in Israel. Although she had considered working in the theater, Megan wanted work that would contribute to society and would affect individuals. In thinking about the jobs she had enjoyed and her own talents, Megan realized that she had enjoyed working with children as a camp counselor. The combination of her social conscience and her experience as a counselor led her to consider teaching.

> I tried to think about what jobs I liked and what jobs I felt I was good at. And I really felt that I enjoyed and was good at being a camp counselor. And I wanted to do something that was with people and would kind of directly make some kind of contribution to society and directly affecting people.

The choice to teach English as a subject came naturally, as Megan felt most competent in this area. She also felt that English allowed a more personal approach to teaching than did other subjects.

> I love English. I love reading books. And one thing about it is that reading and writing can be so personal. Say, more personal than math. To get kids to be able to write well and to communicate well, they have to talk about themselves and write about themselves.

While Megan applied to both journalism school and teacher education, she was first accepted by the teacher education program. Megan decided to attend, and if she did not like it, to go on to study journalism.

Conceptions of Teaching English

Megan's ideas about teaching English centered around the development of writing skills and the encouragement of critical thinking skills through reading. Her focus on the skills of writing and critical thinking reflected her belief that students need these skills to be successful in later life.

> Sometimes I think I don't know why [students study English]. Because they're never going to read a book anyway. You know, it's a dying art. . . . But on the other hand, I just think that to be really successful they need to be able to write and that they're handicapped if they can't . . . it's crucial. And I think . . . kids need to be able to express themselves in writing for a variety of reasons, for whatever job they're going to do, any kind of communication they're going to have.

In addition to developing students' writing abilities, the study of English offered students the opportunity to expand their perspectives and to learn to think critically.

> I think teaching them to think critically through looking at literature will help them in a lot of ways. I mean, kind of on a basic institutional level of the reason of the school, it will help them to be good citizens if they can think critically. I would think it would help them in their personal lives and in their jobs and just to offer them the opportunity to expand their world and their thinking through literature, through seeing different kinds of ideas and opening them up to new ways of looking at things and new ideas.

This conception of English as both skill development and exposure to new perspectives and ideas informed Megan's goals for students, which included enabling students to express themselves clearly in writing, provoking them to look at life and ideas from more than one point of view, exposing them to new ideas, and helping them "feel that reading and writing are avocations of theirs, or interests, or something they are capable of."

Megan emphasized the importance of developing writing skills and self-confidence among her students. "I want students to feel comfortable writing . . . that their writing is O.K., that we'll work on it, but [that] they have good thoughts and if they write them down on paper, it's not going to get slashed up; it's going to get looked at and treated with care." To inspire confidence in student writers, Megan felt that teachers must look first at ideas in writing and later at mechanics. Students must first care about what they are writing in order to want to improve their writing, she believed. In selecting texts for teaching writing, Megan commented, "I like books that let kids write about what they want to write about and then teach them how to make it better, rather than force them into writing about things they're not interested in."

In teaching literature, Megan was most concerned with finding books that were relevant to students' concerns and that they would read. In talking about how she chose books to use in her courses, Megan commented,

> I think about what kinds of issues I think that they're facing and what works of literature will touch those, so that they'll be interested. And I think very carefully about what's going to interest them, and what appeals to them, so they'll read it. Much more than a personal campaign for the classics. . . . Even if it's not something on any college reading list, if it's something I think is well written, that will expose them to new vocabulary and eloquent ways of stating things, and if it's got ideas that are going to grip them.

Megan preferred to teach literature through thematic units to help students understand the connectedness of literature and to give them a sense of "ownership," a term Megan used frequently in talking about her conception of teaching English. Megan attributed the idea of designing thematic units to her professor of English education and outlined the reasons the professor gave for choosing a thematic organization.

> [He said] that it is unifying, which is important for several reasons. First of all, you draw them in and have them find the connection with the theme and then if they're connecting to the theme, then everything else will build on that, rather than saying, "Here's a novel and we're going to read it because it's a good work of literature." . . . And give them a sense of ownership and draw them in, and the literature is going to magnify

> what they already know or expand what they already know. . . . And also, everything is connected, so why not set it up as being connected, instead of doing a grammar unit and then a writing unit and then a novel and then a couple of poems. It's all interrelated so why not teach it that way.

Megan first encountered the concept of "ownership" in her course in curriculum and instruction in English; "one thing we talked a lot about in [curriculum and instruction] last year was giving a sense of ownership for a text." Megan's belief that students need to feel some sense of ownership for both literature and their own writing influenced her choices of both curriculum materials and activities. In introducing a unit on poetry, Megan first asked students to bring in the lyrics to their favorite song. The class then analyzed the lyrics according to some questions Megan had given them, and the student who had brought it in played the song for the class. Megan suggested that the success of this activity related to the students' sense of ownership of their songs: "So I think they really feel a sense of ownership, like this is mine and I'm going to talk about it and we're going to play it and you're going to be quiet while you listen to my song." Megan saw this activity as a bridge into the unit on poetry, because it sidestepped their negative reaction to poetry and provided them with some of the tools they would need to read poetry. She felt that without preparation, students would be unwilling to expend the effort necessary to study poetry.

> One thing that's hard for them is they're not used to stuff not being filled in. They want it all spelled out. They're not that curious to make the extra effort. It's not worth it. So that's why you have to prepare them and give them a sense of ownership, because they have to care about it in order to want to work it out and if they don't care about it, they never will.

This belief in the need to prepare students in advance relates to Megan's ideas about scaffolding, which were also introduced through her curriculum and instruction courses. Megan compared preparing students for literature to opening a door before entering.

> It's like opening up the door before they have to go in. Especially saying, "Imagine you're in this kind of situation. What would it be like and how would it feel?" Rather than just crash right into it never having thought about what it might be like, and that makes this [poem] that much harder to figure out. . . . It probably wouldn't make much sense to them. You need to be prepared for it. Just like you wouldn't give them poly-

> nomial equations before giving them a watchamacallit. . . . I mean you wouldn't jump into the middle of some historical event or scientific experiment without preparation.

The concept of scaffolding was first introduced in relation to the teaching of writing, but Megan used the concept for thinking about teaching both writing and literature. In talking about how she taught her students to write a critical essay, she referred explicitly to her use of scaffolding activities in class. "They wrote the final draft at home and they probably wrote half of their rough draft at home, but there was lot of scaffolding that they did in class." Megan's decision to introduce poetry through the use of song lyrics represents an instance of both scaffolding and the encouragement of ownership, as Megan led them through the process of analyzing poetry in the familiar context of popular music before introducing the more unfamiliar and difficult terrain of poetry. Her dual beliefs in the importance of ownership in teaching English and in the centrality of writing in the English curriculum formed the cornerstone of Megan's conception of teaching English.

Teaching Context

After graduating from her teacher preparation program, Megan found a job teaching English and drama at a suburban, multi-racial high school. Megan taught two sections of "regular" junior English and three periods of drama. Her junior English class was composed of approximately 25 students who, for one reason or another, had not been successful in English. While there was one track below "regular," Megan believed that for all intents and purposes regular English represented "the bottom"; the lower track received more individual attention and remedial help than the students in the regular track.

Teaching *To Kill a Mockingbird*

Megan chose not to teach Shakespeare to her class. She developed a unit on discrimination and prejudice, which she taught to her junior English class. *To Kill a Mockingbird* was the central novel in the unit, which also included an excerpt from the television show "Eyes on the Prize," which focused on the murder of a young Black man and the trial of his accused murderers; a short story by Shirley Jackson, "After You My Dear Alphonse"; a poem by Langston Hughes, "Theme for English B"; and a song about prejudice. In deciding to do a unit on prejudice, Megan said she never considered using a novel other than *To Kill a Mockingbird*, especially since it was typically taught in the junior English classes at her school. In talking about how she developed the unit, Megan commented,

> For me, the criteria of a unit are something the kids can relate to directly, that they all have experience with and they all can find some sense of ownership with the topic. Also something that, some subject that's broad enough to include all the kids in the class, and topical. It also seemed to me with this class in particular . . . this may be the only time in their lives that my students will be together with students of all these different races.

Megan had multiple goals for the unit, including: having students think about prejudice and how things had changed since the time of the novel; helping students to understand the difference between institutionalized discrimination and everyday forms of prejudice; challenging students to examine the prejudices with which they had grown up; helping students to write a good critical essay; encouraging students to read and enjoy a book; and getting students to look more closely at the writing of the novel, particularly the use of imagery and language. An implicit goal underlying many of the others was to get the students to relate the book to their own lives. The one goal Megan felt was not achieved during the unit was engaging students in a closer look at the language of the novel; as she explained, "I always get more interested in the issues and what they think about the issues and having them write about it, than in critiquing it literarily."

Megan acknowledged that she had culled her ideas for this unit from a number of sources, including her curriculum and instruction class the year before, the curriculum library of her teacher education program, other teachers at her school, and a supervisor of English teachers from her teacher education program.

Megan began the unit by talking about stereotyping with regard to gender. She passed out a worksheet—blue for boys, pink for girls—that contained a number of different adjectives and nouns and asked students to write male or female next to the words that they associated with either gender. After discussing the stereotypes that emerged from the worksheet, Megan asked the students to write in their journals about the ways in which they had been stereotyped. On the next day of the unit, Megan showed the class the first episode of "Eyes on the Prize," a public television series on the civil rights movement. The first episode contained a section on the murder of a 14-year-old Black boy, Emmett Till, and the trial of his accused murderers. After the show, Megan pointed out the analogy between the trial of the white men in this episode and the trial of Tom Robinson in *To Kill a Mockingbird*. Afterwards, students wrote in their journals about their reactions to the episode.

After this introduction, Megan focused on *To Kill a Mockingbird*. She had the students read 10 pages a night and "quizzed them to death" on the reading, at the suggestion of another teacher at her school. Despite the quizzes, Megan was discouraged to find that barely half the class finished the novel. Class discussions focused on the themes of growing up, courage, superstition, prejudice, and parenting. Megan often divided the class into groups and had them discuss issues or quotations from the novel. Once, she had groups decide what was most important about a chapter and then had them teach that chapter to the class as a whole. Some of the activities Megan developed for the unit included having students create a time line of Scout's maturation and another time line of their own maturation, develop a parenting license, tell ghost stories from their own childhoods to the class, and write frequently in their journals about the topics they were discussing.

A major assignment for the unit was a critical essay, on which the class spent four or five days. Students had a choice of writing about the relationship between superstition and prejudice in their own lives and in the novel, or writing about a quotation from the novel on the difficulty of understanding another person's existence. Megan spent much of the class time during this period helping students get started on the essay and providing "scaffolding" activities for their papers.

> But there was a lot of scaffolding that they did in class. They made a cluster and then I gave them a sheet with questions on it and each question was pretty much a paragraph of the essay. And then they took that and wrote a rough draft. And they revised in class and stuff and worked on each other's work.

Megan also wrote a model essay to help students envision what the finished essay might look like.

After the class had finished discussing the novel, Megan gave them a final test. She finished up the unit by teaching a short story by Shirley Jackson about a mother's covert prejudice, a poem by Langston Hughes about how his race affected his perspective on his English class, and the Rodgers and Hammerstein song "Carefully Taught," about children being taught prejudice. Megan also brought in newspaper articles about Ku Klux Klan activities, and the class talked about what they could do as individuals to eradicate prejudice. As a transitional activity into the next unit, Megan took the class to the library and had them choose an outside reading book by or about minorities or women, so they could "read something written with the voice of a minority or a woman."

English as a Discipline and English as a School Subject

Megan clearly distinguished between the discipline of English and English as a subject in high school. In talking about what she would expect an "expert" in English to know, Megan composed a portrait of the English expert that closely paralleled the training provided by a college English department. Megan expected the expert to be familiar with the traditions of both British and American literature, including a background in Shakespeare and Chaucer, among others. In analyzing and discussing literature, the expert should be comfortable using terms from literary analysis and should also be a fluent writer. She indicated that the expert should also possess knowledge of the history of the English language and should have a theoretical understanding of English grammar.

This portrait of the English expert barely overlapped with Megan's ideas of what high school students should study in a high school English class. Rather than reading classic works of American and British literature simply because they are classics, Megan believed students should read works that engage them and speak to their own experiences in life. While she would like students to be sensitive to language, Megan did not expect them to use technical terms for literary analysis. Grammar played a minor role in Megan's conception of the high school curriculum; she emphasized that knowledge of grammar does not necessarily lead to improved writing. While literature dominated her portrait of the English expert, Megan placed writing at the core of the high school curriculum. Her vision of writing included much more than the "literary writing" of the English scholar, encompassing personal writing, journals, and letters, as well as critical essays.

A final distinction that underlies Megan's differing conceptions of the discipline of English and English in the secondary school concerns the degree of abstraction required in literary analysis. While she suggested that the English scholar must be capable of identifying patterns and making connections within a text itself in a fairly objective manner, Megan believed that high school students learn to read by making connections between a text and their own experiences; the pursuit of abstract critical analysis becomes secondary to the quest for concrete connections between life and literature. In one interview, Megan suggested that advanced placement level students might be ready to engage in the form of literary analysis practiced by scholars, but she saw this as an inappropriate goal for most high school students.

While Megan's ideas about expertise in English were informed by her undergraduate background in literature, her understanding of English as a school subject developed during teacher education.

Acquiring Conceptions of English as a School Subject

Megan reflected that had it not been for her professional preparation, she would have had to rely on her memories of her own high school experience to guide her ideas about teaching English. She commented on the influence of teacher education in reference to her belief in the importance of teaching literature in thematic units.

> I'd never thought about how to teach English before last summer. It never crossed my mind. And I suppose like 90 percent of most teachers, I just thought about how I was taught it. . . . But [in my experience] classes were organized around courses. I mean I took American literature, British literature, the Bible as literature, the novel, stuff like that. I don't remember it being thematic. Each unit was just whatever the work of literature was. So thematic sounded like a great idea.

Her curriculum and instruction courses provoked her to think about the purposes for teaching English in high school and contributed to her conceptions of teaching English. Her courses and fieldwork confronted her with basic questions about what is important for students to know about English.

> Curriculum and Instruction in English and Curriculum and Instruction in Literature . . . made me think about what I know about English, what's important to know, what I need to know more about. All the different aspects of it, like why even study English, stuff like that. My internship teaching made me think a lot of the same kinds of things: What do I know, what's important to know, what's important for others to know, what makes up English?

While both her field experience and coursework raised questions about what is worth studying in English, her subject-specific courses also provided her with the concepts that were to become the foundations of Megan's beliefs about teaching English: the belief in the importance of student ownership in reading and writing; the concept of scaffolding in instruction; and the belief in a process-oriented approach to writing instruction. Her curriculum and instruction courses and her class in the teaching of writing all introduced her to the recent research on writing as a process and encouraged her to think about teaching writing as a process, instead of focusing on the final written product. The influence of these ideas was evident in Megan's insistence on pre-writing activities, such as brainstorming and clustering, rough drafts, peer editing, and revision, prior to the submission of a final draft.

PLANNING FOR STUDENT LEARNING

Vanessa, Steven, and Megan each entered teacher education with somewhat differing knowledge and beliefs about English and different reasons for teaching. In some respects, what is most startling about their cases is the striking similarities across the three teachers' knowledge and beliefs about teaching English. All three teachers agreed on the importance of helping students make connections between their own experiences and literature and of using a process-oriented approach to writing instruction. All of them discussed the need to provide instructional scaffolding for students in both literature and writing. While subject matter knowledge and apprenticeships of observation were available to them as sources of knowledge, these teachers drew much more from their subject-specific teacher education coursework in constructing their conceptions of the purposes and appropriate practices for teaching English, a finding which will be explored more fully in Chapter 5.

In contrast to the three teachers without professional preparation, these teachers saw the purpose of planning as making subject matter more accessible to students. For Steven, Megan, and Vanessa, planning seemed to revolve around issues of student engagement, particularly through connections between the content and students' lives, and instructional scaffolding. In their planning, the teachers shared assumptions about the need to motivate students to read and write. They did not assume that students would be intrinsically interested in the subject matter of English. Many of the strategies they reported using address directly the need to motivate students. The concept of ownership helped all three teachers understand one aspect of student motivation from a theoretical perspective. In their planning, the teachers also considered the need to support student learning through the structure of activities. Planning, for these teachers, involved building the scaffolding necessary to reach a particular goal.

CONCLUSION

While all six of the beginning teachers in this study were more similar than dissimilar in their educational backgrounds and subject matter knowledge, the two groups of teachers possessed distinctly different knowledge and beliefs about the purposes, curriculum, and students of secondary-school English. The following chapter explores in more detail the pedagogical content knowledge of the teachers and the sources of that knowledge.

4

Sources of Pedagogical Content Knowledge

Part of what determines how teachers plan for and conduct instruction is a conception of what it means to teach a particular subject matter (Clark & Peterson, 1986; Grant, 1987; Grossman, in press; Gudmundsdottir, 1989; Nespor, 1987; Wineburg & Wilson, in press). While a conception of teaching a specific subject may overlap with a teacher's more general educational philosophy, it differs in its focus on the goals for teaching specific subject matter to students of a particular age. For example, science teachers may envision secondary-school science as a way to teach students the vocabulary they will need in further scientific studies; alternatively, they may conceive of secondary-school science as a way to teach students about the processes involved in scientific inquiry (Baxter et al., 1985). These differing visions of what it means to teach science hold different implications for classroom practice. A clear conception of what it means to teach a particular subject can be a powerful legacy of subject-specific teacher education (Grossman & Richert, 1988).

WHY TEACH ENGLISH?
Conceptions of a School Subject

Teachers' conceptions of the purposes for teaching particular subject matter influence their choices both of particular content to teach and of instructional activities with which to teach that content (Gudmundsdottir, 1989; Nespor, 1987). Although beginning teachers may lack the managerial skills necessary to implement their plans successfully, their beliefs about the goals for teaching their subjects become a form of conceptual map for instructional decision making, serving as the basis for judgments about textbooks, classroom objectives, assignments, and evaluation of students. Conceptions of what it means to teach English include teachers' beliefs about the central purposes for studying English, their goals for students, and their beliefs about the nature of English as a secondary-school subject.

While the six teachers discussed in the previous two chapters shared a relatively common understanding of English as a discipline, they differed in their conceptions of English as a school subject and their overall goals for students. Two of the teachers without teacher education, Jake and Lance, made little or no distinction between their conceptions of English as an intellectual discipline and English as a subject for high school students; Jake and Lance saw both college and secondary-school English revolving around the analysis of literary texts. Megan, Steven, Vanessa, and Kate, however, saw secondary-school English less as an occasion for literary criticism and more as an opportunity to encourage self-expression and understanding through reading and writing.

While all six teachers agreed that English comprises the study of both literature and composition, they differed in their assessments of which was the more important component of secondary English. Jake and Lance believed that the central goal of studying English involved learning how to engage in literary criticism; literature formed the core of high school English. In contrast, Vanessa, Steven, and Megan saw teaching students to express themselves in writing as the central purpose of high school English. Even within the areas of writing and literature, however, these teachers' conceptions of and their goals for teaching literature and writing differed dramatically.

Purposes for Teaching Literature

Within the teaching of literature, the teachers differed in their beliefs concerning the importance of close textual analysis and the role student experience should play in literary interpretation. Jake and Lance saw the purpose of teaching literature as teaching students about literary analysis. In their conceptions of teaching literature, the text was the major focus. Their goals for teaching literature reflected their concern for close textual analysis and the techniques of literary criticism. Even when Lance chose to teach a film in his English class, his goals revolved around teaching students the techniques of literary analysis, as he described in his use of the film *The Breakfast Club*. "They were able to understand the categories of literary criticism . . . it's kind of like *explication de texte* again. That's how I want them to do it."

Jake revealed the primacy of the text in his conception of teaching English in his overall goal for his students. He wanted his students to be well equipped to analyze literary texts on their own, once they left his class.

> I was saying to the kids, "When you leave my class, you're not going to take me with you . . . you're going to take *you* with you. So the biggest thing I can teach you is how to deal with literature there on the page. What do you do when you see it on the page? How do you deal with it? . . . So learn to deal with *explication de texte* and things like that. I think it's really valuable. So that's what you should be able to do, is talk about a poem."

Jake's emphasis on the text was also apparent in his goal for teaching *Hamlet* to his senior English class: "*explication de texte*. To show them how every word is important, and to show them how really intricate a play can be."

While literature played a central role in their conceptions of teaching English, Megan, Steven, Vanessa, and Kate saw the teaching of literature less as an exercise in textual analysis and more of an invitation to students to explore both their own experiences and ideas beyond the realm of their personal experience; these teachers' focus was not on the literary text but on the student in relation to that text. This emphasis on communication and exploration of ideas is evident in Kate's comment on the purposes for studying English: "One is developing skills that are necessary, and another is opening themselves up to the things that will enrich their lives." Megan echoed Kate's comments about the role of literature in expanding students' perspectives on the world.

> I would think it would help them in their personal lives and in their jobs and just to offer them the opportunity to expand their world and their thinking through literature, through seeing different kinds of ideas and opening them up to new ways of looking at things and new ideas.

While all of the teachers agreed on the importance of having students analyze texts closely and support their ideas with evidence from the text, they differed in the emphasis they placed on these aspects of teaching literature. Jake and Lance placed primary emphasis on the text itself, while the other teachers saw the text as a springboard for developing skills and broadening students' perspectives. This difference in emphasis was apparent in Steven's decision to have his students forgo reading the actual text of *Hamlet* and in Megan's treatment of *To Kill a Mockingbird*, in which she felt she had neglected "to look more closely at the writing of the novel and look at imagery and language." Another indication of the differing emphases teachers placed on the text appeared in the use of memorization; all three teachers without teacher education required students to memorize passages from Shakespeare, while none of the graduates of teacher education required memorization of literary texts.

The teachers also differed in the role they allowed student experience to play in literary interpretation. While both Jake and Lance recognized the usefulness of having students see connections between texts and their own lives, making this connection did not appear in their goals for teaching literature. Lance argued that students need to learn to "bracket" their own experience while reading literary texts, as he told one of his students as they were reading *Romeo and Juliet*.

> And I just tried to show that, even though this was very different from his own experience of the world, a good way to approach literature is to bracket your own experience of the world, to try to figure out what's going on within the text itself, and then be able to make decisions about it.

In contrast, Megan, Steven, Vanessa, and Kate believed that enabling students to make connections between literature and their own experience was the major purpose for teaching literature at the high school level, as Steven suggested in his philosophy for teaching literature: "I think it's my job to make the connection between the work and their lives." Vanessa echoed Steven's belief in the importance of relating literature to student experience: "But if they can enjoy something and find something that they can identify with and like and learn from and use in their own personal experience, I think that's something that's universal."

The teachers' differing goals for teaching literature surfaced in their approaches to thinking about teaching "The Death of the Ball Turret Gunner," a poem by Randall Jarrell (see Appendix B, Interview #3 for complete text). Jake, Lance, and Kate all concentrated on a close textual analysis of the poem, providing relatively few opportunities for connection to student experience. Lance stated that his major goal for teaching the poem would be to teach students the difference between metonomy (the substitution of a word or name that relates to an entity for the entity itself) and metaphor (an implied and evocative comparison between two dissimilar things) in poetry.

> It would be a good poem to teach the difference between the metonymic level and the metaphoric level of a poem, because it has a really clear and coherent metonymic level. You can just explain what the words are and how they fit together . . . and they would see how a poem works on that level. And it works really well. And that would be interesting for them and then with the metaphoric level thrown into that, that would be a good exercise in learning to interpret a poem.

Jake's goals for teaching the poem also centered around literary analysis: "One reason why I like teaching poetry, it really makes them, it almost forces them, to get into the text." Kate's ideas about teaching the poem also emphasized close textual analysis.

> I may talk a little bit about the title, and how the title relates to the poem, of course, but how that helps it—what the poem would be like without the title. And the choice of specific words such as "hunched"—why does he say "hunched"? Why does he say "fell"? And I would want them to see the parallel between dream and nightmare . . . the word "belly," why the word "belly"?

Rather than starting with the text of the poem, Megan, Steven, and Vanessa stated that they would first try to connect the poem to student experience. Megan commented that she would begin by asking students to think about the loneliest they had ever been.

> I might start out by saying, imagine, what's the loneliest you've ever been, the most isolated? What was it like? Why was it so isolating? What did you feel like? Have them write something about that. . . . And then say something about imagine you were in a ball turret and tell them what that was . . . and then [ask] what it might have felt like to be in a place like that. . . . And then I'd read the poem . . . and then have them talk about it.

Megan compared this kind of preparation for the poem to "opening the door before they have to go in." Steven also discussed the need to connect the poem to student experience: "So what I would do is try to think of a bridge between this piece of literature and their lives." Steven thought he might begin a discussion of the poem by showing students photographs of combat or discussing popular images of war represented by G.I. Joe and Rambo. Vanessa considered using the poem as part of a thematic unit about poems of death or war; in fact, Vanessa later taught the poem as part of a unit on war poetry, which she began by taking her students to see the movie *Platoon*.

Again, the difference in goals for teaching the poem was one of emphasis. Steven, Megan, and Vanessa all mentioned teaching students the skills of poetry analysis as an underlying purpose for teaching the poem; it was simply not their central purpose. The differing goals for teaching the poem led in turn to varying instructional strategies. Kate, Lance, and Jake all claimed they would begin with the text itself, analyzing the poem line by line. Megan, Steven, and Vanessa all created activities to prepare students for the overall theme of the poem.

Both Jake and Lance based their assumptions about teaching literature on their disciplinary knowledge of literature. Jake claimed that his college courses in English influenced both his ideas about English and his ideas about teaching English. Lance's ideas about teaching literature also had their roots in his disciplinary knowledge.

Steven and Megan attributed their ideas about the need to create bridges between student experience and literary texts to their curriculum and instruction courses. Megan reported learning about the importance of preparing students prior to teaching a text through her professor of English education, as well as through practice and discussions with her peers in teacher education. Steven's self-reports of his conceptions of teaching English during his internship experience prior to teacher education resemble closely the conceptions held by Jake and Lance. Although Steven recognized that conducting his high school classes as miniature versions of the English literature seminars from which he had recently graduated was not working, he was unable to reconceptualize the teaching of English on his own. Perhaps because of this prior teaching experience, Steven, of all the graduates of teacher education, most unambiguously attributed his new conceptions of teaching both literature and writing to his subject-specific coursework.

In addition to their contrasting beliefs about the teaching of literature, the teachers also differed in their ideas about the teaching of writing.

Teaching Writing

While all six teachers agreed on the importance of teaching students to write, they differed dramatically in their conceptions of what it meant to teach writing, particularly in their beliefs about the relative importance of structure and content and in their attitudes toward technical correctness. While Jake and Lance believed that students needed to master the forms of writing and stressed the importance of grammar, Steven, Megan, Vanessa, and Kate emphasized the need for students to learn to express their ideas in writing before striving for technical correctness.

One of Lance's major goals for his ninth graders was to teach them to become literate, which for him denoted mastery of grammar and rhetoric. "I wanted them all to be incredibly literate . . . to understand the grammar really well and to be able to use it and . . . to construct papers that . . . work . . . and that don't have any stylistic or grammatical errors." Jake also included grammatical correctness as one of his central goals for the teaching of writing.

> My goals for them would be to write a cohesive, clear, organized paper with no grammatical errors. Never any run-ons or anything like that. . . . So go at it from the technical aspects to begin with for sure . . . obviously getting rid of all the errors you just want to get rid of immediately—the run-ons, the fragments, the parallelism mistakes, and misplaced modifiers—I mean all of those little things.

In contrast to Jake and Lance, the other teachers believed teaching writing consisted of first helping students feel comfortable expressing their ideas in writing; they believed teachers should first focus on the content of the writing and address grammatical correctness later on. As Kate commented, "It seems to me that first they should learn how to express themselves and then learn how to put it in a cleaner way, more grammatically correct." Megan argued, "And they need to learn how to express themselves clearly and in an organized way, and to get them to do that, they have to care about what they're writing about and they have to want to make it understandable."

In large part, these divergent conceptions about the teaching of writing reflect differing beliefs about the relationship between knowledge of grammar and writing ability. Jake and Lance believed that knowledge of grammar helps students write correctly. As Jake expressed it,

> I think they have to know grammar because they have to learn how to write. And you can't know what a run-on sentence is without knowing what an independent clause is. And you can't know what an independent clause is without knowing what a noun and a verb are. You just can't. So that's why they have to learn grammar.

Megan, in contrast, did not believe that knowledge of grammatical rules necessarily made one a better writer. "But in my mind [writing and grammar] don't go together. Knowing grammar doesn't make you a good writer, and I don't want them to think that just because they don't remember parts of speech that they're not good writers, or because they do, that they are."

Believing that knowledge of grammar would improve student writing, Jake and Lance concentrated on grammatical and technical errors in student assignments. Jake corrected every error in every paper he received, saying, "I'm very nitpicky about writing. [I'm nitpicky about] grammar, logic. I don't let the kids get away with anything. The papers are covered with red." In contrast, Steven believed in focusing first on the content of a paper and supporting students' ideas, rather than correcting technical errors. "I could have marked up that paper right and left, but if I were to do that, the student, one, probably wouldn't care, wouldn't look at it, and probably wouldn't make the changes. But if I said, 'This is a good part, I like this one idea, . . . let's go with that.' . . . "

The contrasts between these two approaches to error parallel the contrasts among the teachers' beliefs about the relative importance of structure and content in the teaching of writing. Jake and Lance believed that students need to master the forms of argumentative or persuasive writing; in teaching writing, they emphasized the importance of structure—sentence structure, paragraph structure, and overall essay structure.

Steven, Vanessa, Megan, and Kate believed that in teaching writing, teachers should first help students feel comfortable with expressing their ideas; once students have expressed themselves in writing, they can begin to put their ideas into an appropriate form. As Vanessa asserted, her major goal is to help students feel confident about writing.

> I'd like them to be comfortable with and familiar with the fact that there's more than one kind of writing. . . . I think I would just like them all to be able to come out writing, feeling as if they have a fairly definite style of their own that they feel quite comfortable with . . . when they pick up a pen, not to have any kind of fear. Just to be able to sit down and just say, "O.K., I'm going to write this and I'm going to do the best I can do and I'm going to enjoy it."

This desire to help students feel confident as writers led to an initial emphasis on the content of student writing. By having students write frequently in less-structured writing assignments, these teachers hoped to enable students to become more fluent writers. By assigning topics that students cared about, the teachers believed students would have a personal stake in improving their papers. As Steven suggested in his critique of a composition textbook, he believed that the "nitty gritty" aspects of writing could be addressed once students were hooked into writing.

> This [text] looks fine for getting down to some of the nitty gritty stuff. New paragraph strategies, and introductory and concluding paragraphs, thesis sentences and that kind of stuff. Punctuation principles. The problem is . . . I just can't see passing this out the first day. . . . Because there's so much more to writing than punctuation principles; what a way to start out! I tend to start out to try to hook the kids into writing about themselves, so if they do that, they've got to be hooked.

Steven reiterated his belief that until students cared about what they were writing, they were unlikely to make the effort to polish their papers or to use principles of punctuation in their writing.

The differences between these two approaches to the teaching of writing reflect different traditions in the field of English education. Within one tradition, knowledge of grammar is seen as inextricably connected to writing ability; to help students improve their writing, teachers teach grammatical rules. In a second tradition, teachers are urged to focus not on the written product but on the processes involved in thinking and writing (see Grommon, 1984, for a historical perspective on this second tradition). When research revealed little or no relationship between the study of grammar and writing ability (Braddock, 1963; Elley, Barham, Lamb, & Wyllie,

1979), English educators urged teachers to rethink their ideas about the purposes and strategies for teaching grammar, with varying success (McCaleb, 1979; McEvoy, 1984).

An earlier tradition in writing instruction emphasized the final written product over the writing process. Students were taught certain forms of writing, such as the five-paragraph essay, and teachers emphasized adherence to these pre-established structures. The work of researchers on writing (such as Emig, 1971) countered the notion that writing is primarily a way of ordering already developed ideas and shifted the pedagogical emphasis away from the finished product to the processes writers engage in while writing. In this model, writing is seen as a series of recursive processes from prewriting and drafting through final revision and editing. Initially, writers focus on the content to be expressed; in its early stages, writing can be seen as an extension of thinking. During the processes of revising and editing, writers begin to pay more attention to how ideas are expressed. This model of the writing process suggests a different approach to the teaching of writing: Teachers encourage students first to express their ideas without worrying about the form of writing, then to write and revise their papers with the help of others, and, during the editorial process, to correct errors of grammar and usage.

All six teachers in this study were most likely taught to write within the tradition that emphasized the written product and the importance of grammatical knowledge for writing. Jake and Lance continued this tradition within their own classrooms, relying on their apprenticeships of observation to shape their approach to teaching writing. Jake developed his ideas about the importance of technical correctness through his own apprenticeship of observation as a college English major, as he modeled his approach to teaching writing after a college professor. Lance also used a college composition course as a model for thinking about teaching writing in high school; "just what it's like in freshman English [at his alma mater] . . . is what I would feel they would have to know."

Steven entered teacher education believing that teaching writing consisted of teaching students to diagram sentences. He, Vanessa, and Megan learned a different way to think about teaching writing during their curriculum and instruction courses. In these courses, they were introduced to the research on the writing process, the research on the absence of relationship between the study of grammar and writing ability, and a model of teaching writing that encouraged teachers to concentrate initially on the content of students' ideas, to assign frequent short writing assignments, to put students into peer revision groups, and to require students to rewrite and revise their writing. Steven described what he believed was the main emphasis of all three of his curriculum and instruction courses: "Don't demand that they write flawless essays the first draft and turn them in. Don't assign something and just collect it once and give them a grade, turn it back, and move on to the next assignment. . . . There has to be some process."

Kate provides a discrepant case concerning conceptions of teaching writing, for although she had no formal teacher education, she was exposed to ideas about teaching writing as a process through a friend who was also an English teacher. Kate's goals and ideas for teaching writing ally her with Steven, Megan, and Vanessa; she came to believe in the importance of focusing first on content and then helping students refine their writing.

> I used to think that writing consisted of taking your thoughts, which are already here, and putting them there. And I'm learning that those are not distinct processes. That writing creates thought. So the more I write, the more I find out what I think. That writing can be a form of exploration.

Kate's general goals for teaching and her belief that English centers around communication may have made her more receptive to this conception of writing and writing instruction. In fact, for all six teachers, their conceptions of English, their motivations for teaching, and the contexts in which they taught, both the institutional settings and the particular students, influenced their conceptions of what it means to teach English.

Constructing Conceptions for the Classroom

Jake and Lance both saw English as a discipline centrally concerned with literary analysis; teaching was a way to pass on their own love and enthusiasm for literature. Their subject matter knowledge and motivations for teaching strongly influenced their conception of teaching English as teaching students about literary analysis. Their experience in schools made them aware of the divergence between their own literary interests and the interests of their students; rather than changing their conceptions of teaching English, however, this experience made them resolve to find different students and contexts for teaching.

Kate's conception of English as centered around communication rather than literature, and her motivation for teaching, which revolved not around subject matter but around her belief in personal transformation through education, set her apart from Jake and Lance. Both her conception of English and her reasons for teaching made her more sympathetic to a view of teaching writing that emphasized exploration and development of ideas and to a view of teaching literature that encouraged students' exploration of their own experience. These conceptions of teaching English are consistent with her larger conception of teaching as a stimulus for personal transformation. Kate's goals for teaching both writing and literature ally her more closely with Megan, Steven, and Vanessa than with Jake and Lance, her colleagues without professional preparation. Her classroom practice, however, did not always reflect her more general goals. Her apprenticeship of observation in high school and college provided her with a model of teaching English that focused on the literary text, a model she adopted in her own classroom teaching. This disjunction between her goals and practice was evident in her ideas about teaching "The Death of the Ball Turret Gunner" and in observations of her teaching, during which she focused primarily on literary analysis. Kate seemed to waver between her explicit goals for teaching English and the implicit model for teaching English she acquired through her experiences as a student.

By his own reports, Steven's initial conceptions of English and his reasons for teaching paralleled those of Jake and Lance. Like them, he initially saw secondary-school English revolving around analysis of literary texts, and he wanted to teach primarily to extend his own enthusiasm for literature. His first encounter with teaching changed his motivation for teaching from a desire to pass on his literary knowledge to a desire to work with students. His experience in teacher education, particularly in his curriculum and instruction courses, subsequently helped him restructure his ideas about teaching English. He changed his ideas both about the relative importance of writing and literature and about appropriate ways to teach both literature and writing. The context in which Steven taught supported his newly developed conceptions of teaching English.

Megan's motivation for teaching, like Kate's, focused more on working with students than on working with literary texts. Megan found the ideas presented in her curriculum and instruction courses to be congruent with her own purposes for teaching. The context in which Megan taught (she taught students with little interest or confidence in reading or writing) strongly reinforced the importance of connecting literature to student experience and the centrality of writing in the secondary English curriculum.

The case studies of these six teachers suggest the complex interrelationship among beliefs about teaching, subject matter knowledge, and teaching context in the development of conceptions about teaching English. The teachers' own experiences as students in English classes provided implicit models for the teaching of literature and writing. Even when beliefs about teaching, subject matter knowledge, and reasons for teaching all predisposed a teacher like Kate to a certain conception of teaching English, the apprenticeship of observation proved difficult to overcome in classroom practice. Subject-specific teacher education helped Megan, Steven, and Vanessa break with their prior experience as students and develop new conceptions of teaching English that centered around English as a secondary-school subject. These differing conceptions of what it means to teach English resulted in differing ideas about the English curriculum, both what should be taught and how content should be organized.

WHAT SHOULD WE TEACH?
Selection and Organization of Content

The differing conceptions of English as a school subject expressed by these six teachers paralleled their differing knowledge and beliefs about the English curriculum. As one component of pedagogical content knowledge, curricular knowledge includes knowledge and beliefs concerning the selection and organization of content at different levels of the curriculum. Curricular knowledge for secondary English encompasses knowledge and beliefs about what should be taught in English at various grade levels, knowledge of curriculum materials available for teaching English, and knowledge and beliefs about how courses should be organized. The six teachers in this study differed in their ideas both about appropriate content for particular English courses and about how that content should be organized; the teachers also based their curricular decisions on different grounds.

The six teachers were asked to plan three hypothetical courses: a general-track, ninth-grade English class; a tenth-grade composition course; and a college-preparatory, eleventh-grade American literature class. The teachers were asked about their goals for the courses, their concerns about teaching the courses, and their expectations for students. The teachers were also asked about the content they would include in the courses and how they might organize that content. For the American literature and ninth-grade English courses, teachers were given a hypothetical bookroom list from which to choose texts (see Appendix C). The teachers' responses to these tasks revealed the differing ways in which they thought about the secondary English curriculum.

Ninth-Grade English

The teachers' goals for the freshman English class paralleled their conceptions about the central purpose of secondary-school English: Megan, Steven, and Vanessa stated that they would focus on developing writing skills, while Lance, Jake, and Kate planned to concentrate on the study of literature. These differing goals mirrored the different ways in which the teachers planned to organize the course. Seven and Megan indicated that they would organize the course around the development of writing skills.

Megan commented that she would teach literature in thematic units that would be connected to the students' writing assignments. Steven argued that although he would want to integrate literature in some way, the coherence of the course would lie in the development of writing ability rather than in the study of literature.

> We'll deal with this book and this idea in this book, but really our main objective is to get you to write better and that's what I'm going to be working on. . . . If you look at the whole year, I mean there isn't a whole lot of continuity between these various books that I teach or the concepts or ideas that I try to stress in the course of a unit, but if you look at their writing, that's where things begin to sort of fall into place.

Vanessa and Jake both planned to organize the course by the level of difficulty presented by different genres. Because they felt that short stories would be most accessible to students, they would both begin with the short story, moving on to novels and poetry. While they agree on the importance of organizing the course by level of difficulty, they differed in the emphasis they would place on writing and literature; Jake would emphasize literature, while Vanessa would focus on writing. Both Lance and Kate organized the course around the construct of literary genre. Kate said the organization of the course would be "haphazard," as she saw the purpose of the course as "dabbling" in different literary genres. Lance first wanted to organize the course by genre or literary structure; he then considered the possibility of organizing the course around themes such as visions of utopia, industrialization, and issues of gender, race, and marginality. Lance finally decided to organize the course around the historical development of the novel.

The different organizations the teachers proposed for this hypothetical course are consistent with their conceptions of teaching English. Jake, Kate, and Lance organized the course around the study of literature, while Megan, Steven, and Vanessa organized the course around teaching writing. The similarities between Vanessa's and Jake's ideas for organizing the course also reflect the influence of teaching context on curricular knowledge, as they both taught at the same school.

Interesting differences also emerged among the teachers' choices of texts for freshman English. Certain texts were chosen only by the teachers with teacher education, while others were chosen only by the teachers without professional preparation. For example, the three graduates of professional preparation all chose *To Kill a Mockingbird* and *Reflections on a Gift of Watermelon Pickle*. On the other hand, all three teachers without teacher education mentioned *Great Expectations*, and two of the three selected a Shakespeare play, while neither Megan, Steven, or Vanessa selected these texts. The teachers' choices for the freshman curriculum reflected the different grounds they used in selecting texts.

Steven talked at length about the difficulty of choosing texts that would be appropriate for an entire class of students. Focusing on the fact that the class was identified as a general-track class, Steven commented on the wide range of student abilities commonly grouped into a general track and worried that books that were easy enough for some students might bore other students "to tears." Steven liked the idea of teaching plays because "plays might enable you to get to the point of where you can challenge different kids at different levels." Megan also focused on the fact that the class was described as general track and tried to choose books that the students would find inherently interesting. She commented, "They're a pretty low ability level, and it'd have to be something that they're interested in and that they're going to want to finish." In explaining why she would begin the ninth-grade class with a book such as *Of Mice and Men* or *To Kill a Mockingbird*, Vanessa also stated that her choice of texts reflected her knowledge of what students find interesting or difficult. "I mean, 90 percent of the kids like *To Kill a Mockingbird* or *Of Mice and Men*. But things they have difficulty with, it's hard for them to accept it, and if they've already not accepted it, then it's really hard to get anything done with it."

Like Vanessa, Jake would also organize his course by level of difficulty, but his choices of texts reflected his judgments of literary worth rather than his sense of student response. In choosing the novels for freshman English, Jake described *Great Expectations* as "one of the greatest classics of all times," and *Gulliver's Travels* as "a brilliant novel." Lance's choices of texts were even more firmly grounded in his disciplinary knowledge. He chose texts that were central to the development of the novel, and when asked what books he would add if he could choose anything he wanted, he replied, "I'd want to choose something continental, but everything else is American, Anglo-American, so I don't know if I would do it or not." Lance's concern was for the disciplinary cohesion among the texts; his decisions reflected his knowledge of literature, rather than his knowledge of students.

American Literature

The teachers' goals for their students in the hypothetical American literature class again reflected their overall conceptions of the purpose for teaching English. Steven and Megan mentioned the development of writing skills as the central goal, while Lance and Kate stated that they would want to expose students to different periods in American literature or, as Lance commented, "hit the main books." Vanessa stated her main goals as helping students "to really get enthused about at least one book" and to appreciate good literature, while Jake said he would concentrate on teaching students to write and think critically and on teaching them basic literary theory.

The ways in which the teachers planned to organize the course reflected their differing emphases. Steven and Megan wanted to organize the literature by thematic units that would integrate literature and writing, while Vanessa, Kate, Jake and Lance all planned to organize the literature chronologically. The teachers' decisions about how to organize the course reflected different concerns, as the comments of Lance and Megan illustrate. Lance explained why he would want to use a chronological approach to American literature.

> And because I have the sense—because for me literature is always social—that American authors read American authors, and so that they're basing themselves, at least partially, on what came before. . . . And also because history is important to me. So the issues that you see in one period change or come into life in another period too, and you can kind of keep them together that way, and the texts aren't just floating off and don't just become a language but there has been a grounding.

Lance's reasons for choosing a chronological organization are rooted in his disciplinary knowledge about literature.

Megan chose a thematic organization to help students connect personally to the literature.

> [The units] would be thematic. For a number of reasons. One thing is that I think it's important that they realize that this isn't just school for school's sake. And that they're not reading this book because it's good for them. That they're reading this because there's something there that's got meaning for their lives . . . that way there's some personal attachment to what we're doing. It's not just another book, like I've got my history, my math, and my English. It's got some connection to their own lives.

Megan's grounds for choosing to organize the course thematically are more pedagogical than disciplinary.

In looking at the teachers' choices of possible texts for this course, patterns similar to the choices for ninth-grade English reappear. For example, certain texts, such as *My Antonia*, were chosen only by the teachers with teacher education, while other texts, notably *Moby Dick* and *The Sound and the Fury*, were chosen only by the teachers without professional preparation.

The distinction between texts that are part of the accepted canon of Anglo-American literature and those that fall into the loose category of adolescent literature helps clarify the teachers' curricular choices. When all of the books on the hypothetical bookroom list were categorized as either canonical or adolescent literature, the teachers' choices fell into a pattern. Lance chose the highest percentage of canonical works for both of the courses, while Steven, Megan, and Vanessa chose the highest percentage of adolescent works for the ninth-grade English class. Vanessa, however, selected a large percentage of canonical texts for American literature, consistent with her decision to organize the course chronologically. She and Jake, who taught at a school that provided syllabi for each grade level, had an identical breakdown of canonical and adolescent texts for this course. Megan's and Steven's choices for American literature show a balance between canonical texts and adolescent literature (see Table 4.1).

Ninth-grade English differs from American literature in that it is a pedagogical, rather than a disciplinary, construct; ninth-grade English has no implicit disciplinary structure and no direct analogue in the college curriculum. Megan, Steven, and Vanessa agreed, however, on the central purpose of freshman English as helping students learn to write. They also agreed on

Table 4.1. Percentages of Canonical and Adolescent Texts Selected in Planning Hypothetical Courses.

	Canonical	*Adolescent*
Ninth-Grade English		
Lance	100%	–
Kate	67%	33%
Jake	50%	50%
Megan	29%	71%
Steven	22%	78%
Vanessa	14%	86%
American Literature		
Lance	92%	8%
Kate	71%	29%
Jake	89%	11%
Megan	56%	44%
Steven	44%	56%
Vanessa	89%	11%

many of the texts that they would use in a freshman curriculum. In choosing the curricular materials, Megan, Steven, and Vanessa considered primarily the interests and ability levels of the students. Their agreement concerning choices of texts seems to indicate a pedagogical convergence. While they all believed the central purpose of freshman English is to teach students how to read literature, Jake, Lance, and Kate were in less agreement about the appropriate texts to use. Jake's and Lance's choices, in particular, were based upon beliefs about literary value and worth.

American literature, however, does have an implicit disciplinary structure and an analogue in the college curriculum. In planning for this course, all of the teachers chose a greater percentage of canonical texts; the convergence of curricular choices seems disciplinary in nature, rather than explicitly pedagogical. Vanessa made the most radical shift from ninth-grade English to American literature in her choice of canonical versus adolescent texts. Vanessa's case suggests the influence of context on curricular planning. Her selection of more canonical texts for her hypothetical American literature course mirrors the emphasis of the established curriculum at her school. Megan and Steven, who selected a balance of canonical and adolescent texts, had much more discretion about the texts they taught in their classrooms. While Megan and Steven transferred their beliefs about the need to organize literature into thematic units into their planning for American literature, Vanessa decided to organize the course chronologically, again paralleling the approach of her department.

In part, the different patterns of curricular choices made by the teachers with and without professional preparation reflect the different grounds on which they made their decisions and their different sources of curricular knowledge. Steven and Megan made their choices based on what they knew about students, while Lance and Jake based their decisions on their knowledge of literature. Kate based her curricular choices on what she remembered from her own experiences as a student.

> For novels . . . when I'm answering this right now, I'm thinking more about what tradition says than my actual thinking about it, what I'm about to say. I know that ninth-grade kids often read both *Huck Finn* and *Catcher in the Rye*. I know *Catcher in the Rye* is a big favorite with a lot of kids. I read that maybe in the tenth grade and liked it a lot. . . . *Great Expectations* is not something that I read in high school, but I'm thinking so much of [my selection] is shaped by what I had in high school.

Kate also realized the danger of relying on her own impressions of books from her high school experience: "But I have to be careful because I don't want to just choose what I related to, because other students might relate to other ones."

Kate's predicament suggests some of the dilemmas facing first-year teachers and illustrates the relationship between sources of knowledge and the grounds on which teachers make decisions. In deciding which texts to use in a class, the teachers naturally gravitated toward the texts with which they were already familiar. Kate, Jake, and Lance relied on their disciplinary knowledge and their memories of the books they had encountered during high school. Through their curriculum and instruction courses, Megan, Steven, and Vanessa were introduced to texts that their professor and supervisors felt were appropriate for secondary-school English. By familiarizing prospective teachers with a wider range of titles than they might have encountered in their own school experiences, the curriculum and instruction courses helped broaden the teachers' curricular knowledge. In fact, the texts chosen by all three teachers with professional preparation—*To Kill a Mockingbird, Reflections on a Gift of Watermelon Pickle, My Antonia*, and *The Grapes of Wrath*—were all explicitly mentioned during their curriculum and instruction course. *Reflections on a Gift of Watermelon Pickle* was a required text for the course. *My Antonia* and *To Kill a Mockingbird* illustrate most vividly the influence of teacher education on the teachers' curricular knowledge. *To Kill a Mockingbird* was emphasized in the curriculum and instruction courses as appropriate for high school and was used as the basis for a number of unit plans. *My Antonia* was the topic of a unit plan developed and presented by other students in the course. As none of the teachers had read *My Antonia*, they clearly were not relying on their disciplinary knowledge or apprenticeships of observation. The consistency with which they chose this novel suggests the power of encountering certain texts, presented complete with unit plans, during the process of preparing to teach.

In addition to the booklists and reports of unit plans included in the content of curriculum and instruction courses, the teacher education program maintained a "curriculum library" that included both textbooks frequently used in local high schools and a file of lesson and unit plans developed by teacher education students. Both Megan and Vanessa commented that as first-year teachers, they returned both to their own files of lesson plans distributed through their courses and to the curriculum library for help in developing their own ideas for units.

As these data suggest, teachers can rely on a number of sources in making decisions about the selection of curriculum materials. They can rely on their subject matter knowledge, their memories of what they enjoyed as students, their understanding of students' interests and abilities, and the recommendations of peers and professors. The patterns in the texts chosen by these six teachers, however, demonstrate that in using different grounds for their curricular choices, the teachers also selected different materials. Underlying the teachers' selection of curricular materials is a vision of the students to whom they will teach these texts.

The teachers differed in the extent to which they paid attention to possible variations in student ability level in planning the curriculum for these courses. In the hypothetical planning interview, the ninth-grade English course was described as "general track," while the American literature course was labeled "college preparatory." Both Steven and Megan commented on the fact that the freshman English was labeled general track, and tailored their planning around what they saw as the specific needs of general-track students; Steven talked about the need to prepare for a wide range of student abilities, while Megan discussed the need, in teaching a class that is likely to be unmotivated, to choose works that are inherently interesting for adolescents. Steven, Megan, and Vanessa all commented on the fact that the American literature course was described as college preparatory. One of Megan's concerns in planning the course was "what kinds of things they'll need to be able to do in college." Megan also discussed the particular challenges of teaching students who are college bound, distinguishing their needs from what she saw as the particular needs of the general-track class.

> It's not the kind of situation where I have to pick something so interesting that they'll finally read it after not having read before, but rather that I have to choose something that is going to draw them in and provoke them so that they're going to think about something. That they're not just going to figure out what I want them to think about, but rather that they're going to have their own ideas and own thoughts and figure out ways of stimulating that and getting them to argue things out with each other.

Vanessa integrated information about the level of the course into her goals for the course: "Since they're college bound, they should appreciate good literature."

Of the teachers without professional preparation, only Kate mentioned the described level of the courses; she commented that because American literature was a college-preparatory course, students should know how to put the literature into a historical context. Neither Kate, Lance, nor Jake addressed the description of the freshman English class as general track, although Jake and Kate may not have had an understanding of the term as they both taught in private schools.

The degree to which the teachers with and without teacher education addressed what they saw as specific needs of different students suggests that the teachers may have been planning implicitly for different groups of students. Just as teachers may base their instructional decisions during interactive teaching on a particular "steering group" of students (Lundgren, 1972), teachers may have different knowledge and expectations of students, which influence their curricular knowledge and planning. As Steven commented, before planning for a class, he would first need to figure out "what kind of class I had. Is it college prep? Is it remedial? Where should my focus be?"

WHO ARE THE STUDENTS?

Students' Understanding of English

In order to plan for instruction, teachers must have an understanding of what students already know and what they are likely to find difficult in a specific subject matter. This knowledge of student understanding in a particular content area is another component of pedagogical content knowledge. Knowledge of student understanding differs from more general knowledge of learners in its focus on specific content; the emphasis is not on how students learn in general, but, for instance, how students develop fluency in written expression. Knowledge of student understanding in English includes knowledge and beliefs about students' prior knowledge of literature, language, and writing; knowledge of common difficulties or misconceptions students have in English; and knowledge of how students learn to write and use language fluently and how they come to understand literature.

Knowledge and beliefs about student understanding inform both curricular planning and expectations and evaluations of students (Clark & Peterson, 1986). Yet acquiring knowledge about students' understanding of and interests in English can be difficult. In studies of pedagogical content knowledge, beginning teachers comment on the challenges inherent in trying to understand their subject matter from the students' perspective and to anticipate the aspects of particular topics or content that are likely to prove difficult for students (Grossman & Richert, 1988; Wilson, Shulman, & Richert, 1987). An earlier study indicates that beginning teachers report acquiring most of their knowledge of student understanding from their classroom teaching (Grossman & Richert, 1988), and the teachers in this study are no exception. All six teachers reported learning most of what they knew about student understanding from their teaching experience. Yet the teachers differed in their confidence in assessing student understanding and in the very content and nature of their knowledge and beliefs. The teachers without professional preparation found it exceedingly difficult to anticipate students' prior knowledge and expressed surprise over what students did and did not know. Even after they acquired knowledge of what students found difficult, the teachers did not seem to integrate this knowledge into their instructional plans. In contrast, the graduates of teacher education expressed less surprise over students' knowledge and interests and more confidence in their expectations of students. Furthermore, their knowledge of student understanding was firmly embedded in their conceptions of teaching and their instructional strategies. Finally, the two groups of teachers seemed to have differing implicit assumptions about their students, assumptions that influenced both their expectations for students and their conceptions of teaching.

Jake, Lance, and Kate all discussed the challenges of learning what to expect from their students. Jake talked at length about his difficulty understanding what his students knew, identifying this as the "biggest problem" he faced in his teaching. "It's hard for me to know what they can understand. So sometimes I might be talking, and they might have no idea what I'm saying. Other times it might be really easy for them. I don't know. So that's something that's hard." Kate also expressed her difficulty anticipating what students might find difficult in English: "I don't know yet really. I can think back to what I had difficulty with. Will that help?"

Kate's inclination to think back to her own experience as a student illustrates one of the sources Kate, Jake, and Lance all relied on in developing knowledge of student understanding. All of them used their own memories of their experiences as high school students to help shape their expectations for students, as Jake's comment illustrates.

> I think a hard thing about being a beginning teacher is expectations. What should your expectations be for eighth grade? I don't know. I don't remember when I was in eighth grade. It was so long ago. I've really been trying to think about what I did in eighth-grade English. I have no idea. We did a little sentence diagramming. I remember my teacher's name. That's it. I have no idea.

As Jake's comment reveals, relying on personal experience can be problematic. In Jake's case, he found it difficult to remember accurately his own experiences as an eighth grader. In relying on his memories of his own knowledge of English as a high school student to form his expectations for his students, Lance found himself surprised by what students did not know.

> Well, to my tremendous surprise . . . students have a really hard time just becoming literate. I was surprised. Because I think I was pretty literate. I didn't know literature in high school, but I knew the language.

Lance's surprise illustrates a second danger of generalizing from personal experience. As successful students themselves, the teachers expected their students to be as knowledgeable and as interested in literature as they remembered themselves being in high school. In using their own experiences as students as a template for their expectations of student understanding, Jake and Lance found it difficult to anticipate what students might have trouble with or find interesting. As Jake commented, his own knowledge of literature made it difficult for him to comprehend students' problems.

> One of the things that makes it difficult for me is that my knowledge of literature is a little better than the twelfth graders' or the ninth graders' or the eighth graders', and sometimes it's difficult to see what they're having problems with. That's one of the hardest things. . . . It's difficult to know where they're having problems . . . you take for granted how much you know.

Both Jake and Lance talked about the need to adjust their expectations for students, something they learned through their classroom experiences with students. As they made the transition from college and graduate school to secondary school, Jake and Lance, in particular, confronted the disjunction between their expectations of students, constructed around their own literary knowledge and interests, and the students' knowledge and interests. Lance commented on this transition in talking about teaching *Romeo and Juliet* and his disappointment in the content of the students' final papers.

> I was a little disappointed with the final papers, not terribly, but a little. . . . Just that it was really hard for me to adjust my expectations in the sense that I was always interested in pushing ideas to the extremes, like proving the most obscure theses and showing little nuances in the language that no one had ever seen and why that works. And these kids, of course I know now, wanted nothing to do with that. That was just totally irrelevant to them. And the whole tragedy bit was really pretty obscure for them. And they just wanted to figure out, like they wanted to get the puns and they wanted to know what was going on . . . like what happened and why it was happening and what it meant.

Lance learned through his experience teaching the play that his literary interests and his students' literary interests were not the same. Experience also taught Lance, Jake, and Kate about what students were likely to find difficult. As Kate commented, "Back to the question of what difficulties students have. I guess I found out by doing, where their difficulties are." Lance discovered that students had little knowledge of the English language.

> Splitting infinitives I find really important, because English isn't an inflectional language, it's a positional language, so you have to keep

> positions straight, otherwise the language structure falls apart. But [the students] had no understanding of why English was the way it was and why that was an important point, and also they hadn't any feel that infinitives ought to be kept together.

Through his teaching experience, Jake learned that students had trouble understanding texts that he found easy, such as "The Catbird Seat" by James Thurber.

> Some of [the ninth graders] read that story twice. And they didn't understand a word of it, and that's a fact. I don't know [why they didn't understand it]. I just don't know. And it really upsets me. . . . So again, a good teacher also has to have the ability to see things from a teacher's perspective but also see it from the grade that you are teaching. . . . And that's the hardest thing for me to do.

Jake came to an important insight about the need for a teacher to comprehend the students' perspective on the subject matter. Yet while Jake learned the difficulties of predicting student understanding, he did not learn why students found certain texts difficult or how to make literature more accessible to students. Jake's inability to explain why the students found particular works difficult caused him considerable frustration.

> I can't believe they can't get this [the couplet of a Shakespearean sonnet] after—I can understand reading it and not understanding it, that's fine—but after I point out the three words. Look at these three words. And they all pointed to the reflexivity of the poem. And they couldn't get it. Agghh!! . . . I don't know what to do to help them. For those kids, I don't even know. Sometimes I feel like I'm banging my head against the wall.

Jake's evident frustration illustrates some of the dangers of relying on experience alone for knowledge about student understanding. While Jake, Lance, and Kate learned that their students found particular topics or texts difficult, they could not explain *why*. Without a framework for making sense of how students learn to read literature and to write well, and a repertoire or instructional strategies that support student learning, teachers may find it difficult to learn from experience. In fact, Jake, Kate, and Lance all had trouble learning from classroom experiences alone and integrating their new awareness of student understanding into their instructional planning.

While Lance talked about what he learned about student interests and knowledge of drama through teaching *Romeo and Juliet*, he did not, when asked about how he might teach *Hamlet*, alter his basic approach to teaching Shakespeare. In teaching both plays, Lance chose themes that were central to his own understanding of the play rather than ideas that were likely to resonate with students; his knowledge of literature seemed to overwhelm his newfound knowledge of students.

In thinking about his problems in teaching *Merchant of Venice*, Jake concluded that, in large part, the problem resided with his students. While recognizing that many of the students knew English only as a second language, Jake commented that the students were neither "bright" nor willing to make the effort necessary for understanding Shakespeare. This learning becomes a form of "mislearning," as Jake placed the responsibility for the difficulties of reading Shakespeare on the students. Learning from experience requires that one must first interpret that experience. How Jake interpreted the situation and framed the problem—the students were not bright or motivated enough—colored his solution to the problem—find different students. In fact, both Jake and Lance concluded that they would prefer to teach older students whose interests would be more closely connected to their own.

This problem of interpretation of classroom experience also troubled Kate. When she chose to ignore students' analogies between *A Midsummer Night's Dream* and Disneyland and fairy tales, Kate commented that the analogies were simply attempts to "get her off track." Despite her desire that students connect literature to their own experiences, her classroom experience alone had reinforced her belief that students were trying to divert discussion, rather than making sense of the unknown in terms of the familiar.

Learning from experience is neither as automatic nor as effortless as new teachers might like to believe (Einhorn, 1980; Feiman-Nemser & Buchmann, 1985). While Jake, Kate, and Lance confronted the need to acquire knowledge about student understanding, they had no framework around which to interpret and organize their insights. While experience confronted the teachers with challenges to their prior expectations of students, in order to learn from the experience the teachers first needed to frame the problem for themselves (Schön, 1983). How the teachers framed the problem of student understanding, however, led to instances of mislearning. Jake "learned" that his students were not bright enough to understand Shakespeare. Lance learned that his students were not as literate as he remembers himself being. Both Jake and Lance learned that they could not teach literature on the same level at which they understand it. While these lessons may reflect the realities of their classrooms, they did not help Jake or Lance learn more about teaching English. Their inability to reconceptualize their subject matter knowledge for teaching, even once they recognized the need to do so, may help account for their quick decisions to leave teaching.

While Steven, Megan, and Vanessa also reported learning about student understanding through their classroom experiences as both students and teachers, they seemed to learn different things about students and to hold different expectations about students' prior knowledge and interests. Perhaps as a result of their prior teaching experience during teacher education, these teachers expressed relatively little surprise over what students did and did not know. Most of their comments about student understanding appeared in the context of explanations of curricular or instructional choices, as Megan's comments about teaching poetry illustrate.

> One thing that's hard for [students] is they're not used to stuff not being filled in. They want it all spelled out. They're not that curious to make the extra effort. It's not worth it. So that's why you have to prepare them and give them a sense of ownership, because they have to care about it in order to want to work it out and if they don't care about it, they never will.

While Kate's, Lance's, and Jake's expressions of knowledge about student understanding took the form of discrete observations or comments, Steven's, Megan's, and Vanessa's knowledge of students was embedded in their instructional plans and goals. All three teachers commented on the instructional implications of their knowledge of student understanding. In contrast, even once Jake understood that Shakespeare and poetry were difficult for his ninth graders, he still had trouble conceptualizing what he could do as a teacher to make the literature more accessible. Megan, however, tied her knowledge of students' difficulty with poetry to an understanding of how to help students overcome those difficulties.

What is perhaps most striking about the graduates' comments about student understanding is their consistency with what the teachers learned during teacher education. Unlike Jake and Lance, Steven, Vanessa, and Megan did not assume that the students would find the literature intrinsically interesting. This perspective on students was emphasized during their curriculum and instruction classes, as was the concept of connecting literature to personal experience. What the teachers learned about students' writing ability also reflects the emphasis of their curriculum and instruction courses. Megan commented on students' problems in expressing themselves in writing and the instructional implications of these difficulties.

> The students I have, they've got good ideas but they come out like a three-year-old's. And they need to learn how to express themselves clearly and in an organized way, and to get them to do that, they have to care about what they're writing about and they have to want to make it understandable.

Megan's analysis is entirely consistent with the framework provided by her curriculum and instruction courses, which emphasized the importance of student ownership in writing.

Just as interesting as what Steven, Megan, and Vanessa learned about student understanding is what they did not learn. While Jake, Lance, and Kate all mentioned students' difficulty with grammar, the three graduates of a teacher education program that de-emphasized the importance of grammatical study never discussed this topic.

Teacher education can provide a framework that shapes what beginning teachers subsequently learn from experience. The frameworks Megan, Steven, and Vanessa were exposed to for the teaching of writing and literature provided both a language and philosophy that helped them interpret student misunderstandings and difficulties. Megan, for example, discussed students' resistance to poetry with respect to their need to feel some ownership for the work, while Steven talked of the need to "hook" the students into writing. These frameworks, which will be discussed at greater length in Chapter 5, helped these beginning teachers interpret their students' difficulties within a larger conception of how students learn to write and read.

Without these frameworks, learning from experience can be haphazard, idiosyncratic, and even misleading, as Jake's and Lance's experiences illustrate. Learning that a teaching strategy does not work is not the same as learning what to do about it. Jake's, Lance's and Kate's difficulties in learning from experience were exacerbated by the relative isolation in which teachers work. These teachers had no one with whom to test their interpretations of student difficulty.

A final difference in the knowledge of student understanding between these two groups of teachers concerns their implicit conceptions of students' ability and motivation. While Lance, Jake, and Kate saw themselves ideally teaching students who were bright and motivated, Megan, Steven, and Vanessa presupposed that their students would be of average ability and less than motivated. In essence, these teachers planned for instruction with different "steering groups" (Lundgren, 1972) of students in mind.

Assumptions About Student Ability and Motivation

Kate, who worked in a college-preparatory school with bright, motivated students, chose not to teach in public schools because of her desire to work with students who wanted to learn. Jake decided that if he were to continue to teach, he would prefer to teach at the college level.

> College teaching is not high school teaching. . . . In my college, people wanted to learn. That's not the way it is here. That's part of the reason why I don't like being a high school teacher. Because that's just not my

> bag, to make people do their homework. It's like screaming at people to do their homework. That's just not teaching.

Like Kate, Jake did not see motivating unmotivated students as part of his job. Lance, who would like to see teaching as a Socratic enterprise between a knowledgeable teacher and motivated students, also came to the conclusion that he would prefer to teach older students.

In a very real sense, Kate, Lance, and Jake had an elite group of students in mind as they thought about teaching. Part of their inclination to work with bright, motivated students reflects their desire to deal with the subject matter of English in a way that they find intellectually challenging. Jake commented,

> But I still would rather teach literature in the way I want to teach it, which is more of the way I was taught, which is doing *explication de texte*. Which is, when you talk about something, you take plot as a given. . . . No one has to tell me that at the beginning of *Hamlet* there's a ghost and the ghost says, "Oh, I was killed. Get revenge." Some of the kids here, they have problems at the beginning. They have problems even figuring out what's happening plotwise. . . . I spent a long time just saying basic things . . . who wants to talk about plot? . . . I want to teach people who have better aptitude, and just better knowledge, better background. I think that will be more interesting.

In contrast, Steven, Megan, and Vanessa seemed to have a different type of student in mind. As Vanessa suggested in her comment on students' resistance to Shakespeare, "It's really difficult for the average high school student to really love Shakespeare." Vanessa used the average high school student as her point of reference. Megan's comments about students also suggest that she presupposed her students to be relatively unmotivated. Even in her discussions of the hypothetical college-preparatory American literature class, Megan talked about students' resistance to reading literature. Steven responded to the definition of the class as college preparatory by suggesting that college preparatory can include a wide range of students, including those who are headed for a university and those who are headed for a community college; in making his curricular choices, Steven made sure that the texts would be accessible to the latter group. Steven's comments about the hypothetical freshman English class portray a similar pattern: "General track, they're probably going to be low ability. Don't have any expectations for them. Come in, get them writing, try to hook them with some writing."

These differing images of students help explain the teachers' varying expectations for students, which appeared in both their curricular planning and instructional goals. Megan and Steven seemed to have relatively low expectations for students. In talking about his expectations for students of a hypothetical tenth-grade composition course, Steven commented,

> Prior expectations are frequently thrown right out the window on your first couple assignments. So I'd go in and as for what they'd be able to do, very little is what I would expect. And be pleasantly surprised later on, perhaps, but we'll start out with fairly low expectations.

In selecting texts, Steven chose six of the same books for both the general-track freshman course and the college-preparatory American literature course. The overlapping titles included *To Kill a Mockingbird, My Antonia, Fahrenheit 451, Huckleberry Finn, Reflections on a Gift of Watermelon Pickle*, and *Points of View*. Lance also chose a number of the same texts for both courses, but his overlapping books included *Moby Dick, The Sound and the Fury, The Scarlet Letter, The Grapes of Wrath*, and *Huckleberry Finn*. In essence, these divergent curricular choices presupposed different levels of student ability, as Steven's overlapping titles are considerably easier to read than are Lance's.

To a certain extent, the teachers' differing expectations of students reflected their different teaching contexts. Megan and Steven both taught in public schools with a wide range of students; neither taught students in the highest track, and Megan taught students in the lowest academic track, except for remedial students. In contrast, Vanessa, Kate, and Jake all taught at small independent schools with a narrower range of student ability. One way to look at these data, then, is to look at the fit between the teachers' expectations and the contexts in which they taught.

A competing explanation for the differences in the teachers' expectations, however, concerns the teachers' preparation for teaching. While working at the same school, Jake and Vanessa held different knowledge about and expectations of their students. While Jake commented over and over again about his surprise at what the students did not know, Vanessa never mentioned surprise or dismay at the students' knowledge, or lack of it. While Vanessa began with the assumption that students would lack motivation and that teachers would need to make literature accessible to students, Jake assumed that students would be motivated and would find the literature as interesting as he did.

Even prior to her professional preparation, Vanessa worked with remedial students in both an independent reading center and as a teacher's aide in a local public school. These experiences may have made Vanessa more sensitive to the needs of less able students. Yet her professional preparation also stressed the teacher's responsibility to consider the wide range of student ability in planning for instruction, a lesson that Vanessa, Steven, and Megan all seemed to have absorbed. In contrast, Jake argued that his students' lack of intellectual ability made it even more difficult for him to understand their problems. "But the kids just aren't that bright, a lot of them, and that's very difficult for me."

While Kate, Jake, and Lance seemed to presuppose students from the top tracks—students very much like they remembered themselves being—the graduates of teacher education specifically geared their instructional plans toward less academically inclined students. Even in planning a college-preparatory course, Megan and Steven discussed students' reluctance to read and write. While the teachers without professional preparation risked ignoring the needs of students with less academic ability, Megan and Steven, in particular, ran the risk of not challenging the ablest students.

Knowledge and beliefs about students lie at the heart of teachers' implicit theories and beliefs about teaching (Clark & Peterson, 1986) and may exert considerable influence on teachers' instructional planning and classroom practice. The experiences of these six beginning teachers illustrate some of the sources from which teachers constructed beliefs and knowledge about student understanding in English. While all the teachers cited experience as the primary source for this body of knowledge, Jake's experience, in particular, illustrates the potential for learning miseducative lessons from classroom practice.

As no program of teacher preparation can teach prospective teachers all the knowledge and skills they will need during their teaching careers, one function for teacher education is to prepare teachers to learn from further classroom experience (Feiman-Nemser, 1983). In this particular instance, teacher education transmitted a general lesson concerning teachers' responsibility to reach a wide range of students, as well as specific frameworks with which to make sense of students' difficulties in writing and literary interpretation. What the graduates of teacher education learned from classroom experience was, in part, defined by what they had learned during their professional preparation. The following chapter details both the content and the instruction of the subject-specific coursework that influenced the development of the graduates' pedagogical content knowledge.

5

Mapping Back: *The Role of Subject-Specific Teacher Education*

As teachers are reluctant to acknowledge professional coursework as a source of pedagogical knowledge (Grossman & Richert, 1988; Lanier & Little, 1986), mapping knowledge back to teacher education can be a risky business. In this chapter, I concentrate in great detail on both the content and instruction of the curriculum and instruction courses, as the professor modeled the kind of teaching he wanted his students to adopt in their own classrooms. The details also serve as a snapshot of what goes on behind the all-too-often closed doors of teacher education classrooms. As teacher educators and researchers of teacher education, we need more detailed descriptions of both what teacher educators teach and how they teach it.

CURRICULUM AND INSTRUCTION IN ENGLISH:

First Day of Class

The first meeting of the summer course opened with introductions; the professor introduced himself and then briefly described the course as "a crash course in survival for the fall." The 26 students and 2 supervisors then introduced themselves, talking about their desire to teach literature and creative writing, their own experiences as students, and the quality of their own educations. Remarking that the diversity in this class would almost mirror the diversity they would find among their own students in the fall, the professor then returned to a description of the class and its requirements. He commented that the "course puts a lot of emphasis on activities . . . activities both in and outside of class." In going over the reading for the course, he described the major textbook as "kind of a cookbook of activities. Students found it very useful last year, especially when they got their own classrooms." Outlining the assignments for the course, the professor mentioned that the major assignment for the course—a unit plan—would be due in the fall quarter "so you can tie it into whatever teaching assignment you get in the fall." Reiterating his emphasis on practical activities, the professor commented, "This is primarily an activity course. Unlike other courses that are concerned with scholarship, this one is more concerned with classroom survival." He then launched into a description of the requirement that students keep "learning logs" throughout the quarter.

> For the learning log, there's no set format. Teachers will read to respond to your ideas, comments, and questions. It won't be graded and it will be open-ended. There are no set topics. You can use it to talk about what was interesting in class. . . . This is a chance to tackle new ideas you encounter in the course. Treat it as something useful for yourself.

The professor mentioned that the course encompassed topics that are central to the teaching of English. "Each group is different . . . but these are general broad topics that are always part of the teaching of English."

Following these introductory comments, the professor told the class, "Let's jump in. One question we'll return to again and again is what is English? . . . Let's generate a list of all the different things you've done in English classrooms." The students compiled a list that included creative writing, vocabulary, literature, spelling, grammar, oral recitation, oral reading, film study, expository writing, argumentation, moral issues, poetry, and writing. While students dominated the discussion, tossing out different activities and topics, the professor interjected his own questions: "How about letters? Did you ever have to write letters?" "Any of you ever have telephone skills in English?" "How about interviewing, oral history? They're all part of English courses and textbooks." After generating a list of possible topics and activities on the board, the professor commented, "What is English, when you look at this huge conglomeration? And there are others. But what you face is what to do, what fits together, what has coherence, what do you do and how can you defend it to the department chair and parents." The professor then handed out a excerpt from a piece entitled "Abolish English," describing it as "an old piece but still current in the issues it raises." After asking students to read the passage to themselves, he told the class,

> What I'd like to do is to put you in groups. Your task is to draft a one-page rationale for the high school English program. Think of it as a response to [the author of "Abolish English"] or a response to a PTA newsletter in which someone has raised this question. . . . It should be a coherent rationale for why to teach English. What are you going to

teach? Convince people not to abolish English. . . . This is the kind of thing most English departments have, a one-page description of what they have, what they see their department as.

The students then broke into six groups of four to five people, as directed by the teacher. Groups discussed reasons for teaching English, which in one group included the need to teach communication skills; they all agreed that English offered a way "to find out about the past and to meet the needs of a changing society." This group also asked themselves, "What about grammar? What use is grammar?" The professor circulated around the groups and reminded them: "What's important is your own image of what English is."

After 25 minutes of small-group work, the professor reconvened the class. Instead of talking about the content of the groupwork, however, the professor told the students that he wanted them to put what they had drafted on hold, commenting, "I want you to switch heads now. You've been students for over an hour. Now I want you to think as teachers. First I lectured for awhile and then put you in groups. What assumptions was I making as a teacher in putting you in groups?"

After a moment of silence, students responded, "We could work in groups without any instructions." "We were motivated." "You didn't have to assign groups." After a few of these comments, the professor asked, "Think back to the way I got you started. What assumptions was I making?" Students commented that the professor had assumed that they could read and write. When he asked what assumptions he did not make, they replied that he had assigned a topic and limited the size of the groups. The professor probed students for reasons he might have had in mandating groups of four or five. After students generated a few reasons, he commented: "Part of it is conflict. Smaller groups might agree with each other. This exercise works best if there are two different camps." The professor then asked students what he had done to help them get started and what some of the problems of the groupwork were. Students mentioned the noise, the problems inherent in choosing whom to work with, the problems of staying on task. The professor elaborated on their comments, finally stating, "In some ways, what I did was a very bad example of what you should do in your classes. I sent you off with very little structure and made a lot of assumptions about your ability to do the work."

The discussion continued in this vein, with students commenting on assumptions the professor had made and the professor identifying problematic aspects of his use of groupwork. The class discussed problems with transitions between whole class instruction and groupwork; the professor remarked that it took two-and-a-half minutes to reconvene the class, "quite a long wait time." The professor ended by warning the class that they had to "think in advance" about some of the potential problems and to structure activities to counter some of the possible pitfalls. He commented that throughout the summer they would be examining both content and pedagogy. The professor also identified the challenge the students faced in connecting their rationale for teaching English to classroom realities. Finally, the professor assigned homework: to write a profile of a fellow student, which he described as a high school writing assignment.

This introductory class, while not focused on the specific content that would occupy students for the rest of the summer, foreshadowed a number of specific features of the curriculum and instruction sequence that help account for its influence on how its graduates thought about and taught English. In this class, the professor integrated theoretical concerns with practical realities; modeled activities for the high school classroom, such as learning logs and small-group writing assignments; directly addressed the apprenticeships of observation that students brought with them to class; and provided an example of self-consciously reflective practice.

Course Content

The content of the first quarter of the curriculum and instruction sequence revolved around what the professor described as "a potpourri of different parts of the English curriculum." According to the syllabus, the content included six major topics: the writing process, responding to student work, structuring assignments, language and dialect, teaching literature, and the English curriculum. These six topics break down into the three areas of the English curriculum: writing, language, and literature. The core of the course content revolved around conceptions of writing and writing instruction. Approximately 43 percent of class time focused directly on issues related to writing instruction, while 33 percent addressed issues related to the teaching of literature. Writing was also the first topic addressed in the course. Both its position in the syllabus and the amount of time spent on the topic suggest that issues related to the teaching of writing occupied the center of the curriculum.

For each major area of English, the course introduced both frameworks for thinking about teaching the subject and practical strategies and ideas for the classroom. In the area of writing, the professor presented two conceptual frameworks for thinking about both writing and the teaching of writing. By the end of the second class, the term "writing process" was introduced and the general stages outlined; the professor told the class he was using the vocabulary of the National Assessment of Educational Progress, which uses the terms "generating, drafting, revising, editing, and sharing" to describe the general processes of writing. The professor first described each stage and then focused on the different knowledge and skills necessary during each stage of the writing process. During the fourth week, the professor introduced the concept of "instructional scaffolding" and its five criteria: "ownership, appropriate difficulty, structure, collaboration, and transfer of control."[1]

At the same time these conceptual frameworks were being developed, however, the class also engaged in a wide variety of hands-on activities, including working on a group writing assignment, writing a profile, reading a draft of the profile aloud in "readabout" groups, and responding to student papers. The professor intentionally interwove theoretical discussions with practical involvement

> because any of their understanding of the other [theoretical issues] has to come out of that practical involvement. All of the things I do tend to work that way. It starts with the overall conceptual thing—a mini-lecture for the first 15 minutes or so, then I quickly get them involved in some hands-on activity that we can then come back and discuss in terms of the overall framework that we're working on—the more general concepts. At that point, they usually have a lot more to say and a lot better understanding.

PRINCIPLED PRACTICE:
The Integration of Theory and Practice

One way to analyze the content of the course concerns the breakdown of theoretical issues and practical strategies. Although the professor described the course to students as "a crash course in survival for the fall," he spent a good deal of time outlining the theoretical knowledge and assumptions underlying various instructional strategies and providing both a historical and scholarly context for classroom practices in the teaching of English. Class topics were always related to practical dilemmas and strategies, but much of the actual discussion focused on theoretical issues underlying particular practices. While the topic of one class—how to put assignments together—was practically oriented, the content was conceptual, as the model of instructional scaffolding and its intellectual underpinnings were intro-

[1]Instructional scaffolding is a theoretical model of teaching and learning in the areas of reading and writing (Langer & Applebee, 1986). This model, which draws upon the work of Bruner and Vygotsky, emphasizes the importance of a collaborative relationship between learner and teacher, in which the teacher provides sufficient support and structure to enable students to accomplish tasks they could not accomplish on their own.

duced and developed. In talking about the teaching of literature, toward the end of the course, the professor discussed historical traditions of the teaching of literature and elaborated the model of literature as a transaction between the reader and the text; again, the discussion focused on a conceptual framework underlying specific instructional practices.

The theoretical content of the course, however, was interwoven with practical ideas and strategies for teaching literature, language, and writing. A number of possible assignments, from learning logs to group writing assignments to alternatives to book reports, were modeled and developed during class time. Students constructed both lessons and units that they could use in their own classes and responded to actual student papers. The professor and supervisors urged them to focus on developing materials that they could actually use in their classrooms in the fall. The final assignment of the quarter involved developing a unit of instruction designed around the particular class in which they would be teaching. Throughout the course, the professor reminded the class that they would be facing real students and very real dilemmas in the fall.

This alternation of the practical and the theoretical continued throughout the course. The conceptual frameworks were related to classroom practices, just as instructional strategies were analyzed in relation to the theoretical assumptions of the course. Theory and practice functioned as a double helix, in which the two aspects played off each other, spiraling toward an integrated whole. The professor tried to create a necessary tension between the pull toward the practical and the push to make sense of classroom practice from a theoretical perspective.

> In the summer I'm probably pulling more toward the practical because I have a much better sense of what September's like. And they have not much sense of what kids or schools are like, not much interest in the practical. Our students in particular tend to come from academic places; they have very highly developed academic interests. So the pull there is probably more trying to pull them down to practical things. By this time of year [January] they desperately want very practical things, and I'm trying to pull them back up at that point, trying to get them to make sense of the things they're doing day to day.

Underlying this alternation of the conceptual and practical is an image of "reasoned practice," or, as the professor termed it, "principled practice." The professor reiterated the need for teachers to understand the reasons behind their instructional choices, to be able to explain *why* they do what they do. In talking to the class about strategies to help students with writing assignments, he commented, "We have to think about *why* we make the choices we make, *why* we ask students to do things. There's a lot from the teachers' bag of tricks you can use. You don't need to come up with a completely new methodology for teaching these things. But you need to rethink them." The next week he reiterated the need for a rationale for classroom practice in relation to the teaching of grammar.

> You're going to have to teach grammar in a number of circumstances. That's fine. But you need to think of *why* you are teaching it. How can you teach it in useful and interesting ways? How can you separate it in your own mind from teaching writing?

This emphasis on principled practice was apparent from the very first small-group assignment on the first day of class, in which students were asked to draft a rationale for *why* English should be taught, and persisted throughout the course. "Principled practice" implies that while there are no absolute answers or sure solutions to most of the dilemmas of teaching, teachers must try to connect their choice of instructional activities to their understanding of the underlying purposes for teaching English. In describing the summer course, the professor referred to his desire to develop this perspective in his students.

> There are few answers, lots of problems. By and large, problems that they can come to different solutions to without being wrong. It focuses on why they're doing what they're doing and giving them the sense that in the classroom there are a whole lot of different whys that come into play that can lead to different solutions. That probably causes a bit of frustration in the beginning because they want answers about how to do it. They get used to it.

The graduates of this course acknowledged the emphasis on principled practice. As Vanessa commented, the course "made us think about why we were teaching English and what we wanted them to get out of it, and the goals, all the things that we thought were important."

Inherent in this emphasis on principled practice is an image of the teacher as a professional who must exercise judgment in a complex environment. In fact, much of the course, both implicitly and explicitly, functioned as a form of professional socialization.

Professional Socialization

The content of this course, both the specific topics covered and the stance taken toward teaching as principled practice, served the function of socializing these prospective teachers into the profession of teaching English. This socialization included inculcating a sense of both the history of the profession and the nature of professional responsibility, as well as providing students with a technical vocabulary and a body of specialized knowledge.

During the early sessions of this course, the professor referred explicitly to professional organizations and responsibilities. On the second day of class, he spent five minutes describing the activities and publications of the National Council of Teachers of English, while membership forms for the organization were being distributed. He urged students to subscribe to *English Journal*, a journal of the National Council of Teachers of English, describing the magazine as a good source of "teaching ideas, even things you can use directly in your classroom." When returning the students' first writing assignment, the professor commented on the need for them, as English teachers, to be meticulous about their grammar and spelling.

> As English teachers, you're really on the spot. One way to get in trouble with parents and administrators is careless errors. . . . This turns up in newspapers, literally. "Look, even teachers can't spell or punctuate." You need to be hypersensitive about that sort of thing. Get a spelling dictionary. . . . I don't want to belabor it, but you need to watch it.

These references to national organizations and the representation of one's profession through writing underscored the professional identification and responsibilities of teachers of English.

The professor also made frequent references to history and traditions within the field of English education, setting both concepts and strategies within an historical context. When the class generated a list of possible strategies to help students during each stage of the writing process, the professor commented on their relationship to the tradition of English teaching.

> [Modeling] is an old part of English teachers' repertoire which has been out of favor for a while but is now creeping back in. It used to be *the* way to teach writing. . . . A lot of traditional activities in English classes start with a stimulus. It gives them something to think about, a type of stimulus.

During his discussion of approaches to teaching literature, the professor provided a brief history of the teaching of literature during the twentieth century. This emphasis on historical context again contributed to professional socialization, as the prospective teachers were encouraged to see themselves as part of a larger tradition.

The course also transmitted norms of professional collegiality, in that students were encouraged to collaborate on assignments and to share ideas and activities. The unit plans, writing assignments, and other activities developed by students, often working in groups, were distributed to the class as a whole. Students brought their own classroom problems to class, asking other students for ideas on how to get high school students to read a whole novel or to rewrite an assignment. As the professor described it, "There's a lot of sharing of ideas, what works and doesn't work, among the students. That's one of the tensions of the course—how to provide enough space for that, without being just that kind of exchange."

Perhaps the most important aspect of the professional socialization provided by this course involved the transmission of both a technical language and a specialized body of knowledge, two dimensions of professional culture that Lortie (1975) identified as absent from teaching and teacher education.

> Teaching is not like crafts and professions, whose members talk in a language specific to them and their work. Thus the absence of a common technical vocabulary limits a beginner's ability to "tap into" a pre-existing body of practical knowledge. Without such a framework, the neophyte is less able to order the flux and color of daily events and can miss crucial transactions which might otherwise be encoded in the categories of a developed discourse. Each teacher must laboriously construct ways of perceiving and interpreting what is significant. That is one of the costs of the mutual isolation which attends the absence of a common technical culture. (p. 73)

In this course, the terms surrounding the concepts of writing processes and instructional scaffolding served as a form of technical language; their use by the professor, supervisors, and students ensured a common language with which to talk about the teaching of writing and literature. By introducing the technical terminology related to the processes of writing early in the summer, the course provided a way for students to talk and think about writing from a particular perspective. Part of the professor's intention was to build a common vocabulary for talking and thinking about the teaching of English.

> I'm trying to build a theoretical framework for them that lets them make sense of all the different things they'll encounter, with the different materials they'll have, and at the same time a lot of hands-on experience working with materials, learning how to talk about the kinds of things they'll be doing with their students, how to talk about a writing assignment, how to think about the problems it will pose for students, how to think about the different responses they might give.

In talking about what coursework might add to teachers' developing knowledge of teaching, the professor again referred to the theoretical frameworks: "What it would add beyond simply the experience in the classroom, if it works, would be simply that set of superordinate concepts and frames to make sense of teaching."

The language of writing processes and instructional scaffolding became a repository for these theoretical frameworks. Early in the summer, students began using the terminology themselves, as they talked about writing instruction. By the third week of class, students started to use the terms "generating," "freewrites," and "drafting," during class discussions. One student volunteered, "Freewriting could be drafting, but you can also use it for generating." The professor responded by providing a more precise definition of freewriting, again pushing for a common understanding of these terms: "Freewriting in the literature is one of those terms that gets sloshed around. The traditional use is generating for others, an impromptu first draft." When a student suggested that high school students read their papers to each other to help them with the editing process, the professor responded by renaming the technique: "Peer editing. That's probably my favorite. It's so hard to see your own mistakes." In the interchange of ideas between professor and students, a common language was being constructed.

Student comments support the idea that the terminology covered in class functioned as a technical vocabulary. In his position paper on the reasons for teaching literature, turned in at the end of the second quarter of the sequence, one student commented,

> The discovery of my own rationale of teaching literature (why and how) has been a process much like a student's experience in "learning" grammar—he/she knows most of the rules but lacks the metalanguage to label them. In the same sense, my reasons for teaching literature have not changed since I began C & I. Only now, they are more clearly defined because of Internal Scaffolding, Bruce Miller, the California Literature Project, *Inside Out*, and other C & I related concepts and people.

The acquisition of a common language was also apparent in the persistence with which the terms "ownership" and "scaffolding" appeared in the interviews with graduates of the course.

In addition to a common technical language, students were acquiring a specialized body of knowledge concerning the teaching of English. The pedagogical content knowledge transmitted through this course revolved around conceptions of teaching English; knowledge of students' understanding in English; knowledge of instructional strategies for teaching language, literature, and writing; and knowledge of the secondary school curriculum in English.

Much of the content of this course focused on conceptions of teaching English. While the professor always presented alternative frameworks for thinking about teaching writing, literature, and language, he made clear his preference for a particular approach. In the short unit on language, the professor contrasted two distinct conceptions of teaching grammar—the medical or prescriptive image and the developmental image. He described the medical approach as focused on deficits: "When something goes wrong you need to go in and fix it." In contrast, he defined the developmental approach as based on the presumption that children have their own intuitive sense of grammar, which may be different from adults' sense of grammar. As he described the two conceptions in class, he also played out their differing goals and instructional implications.

> If you have developmental kinds of assumptions, instead of skill and drill, deficit mode, remedial work, you're likely to put much more emphasis on language play, on a rich language environment to give kids a chance to test hypotheses. . . . Both images have the same goals. Both sets of teachers are trying to get to fluent, correct language. But they differ on how they believe language is learned and how teachers can help students learn.

The professor also explicitly outlined his own preference.

> At this point, I don't think my bias is any secret in how I think language should be learned. But let me put context around the medical model, the most traditional approach, and why I don't think it works so well. First, it doesn't work. Lots of people have tried to prove that knowing rules helps people write. There's an intuitive sense that it should.

In a similar fashion, the professor outlined different conceptions of what it means to teach literature—a conception that focuses on the text and a conception that focuses on the transaction between the reader and the text. In literature, language, and writing, the professor posed alternative conceptions of what it means to teach each area of English and the instructional implications, while offering a clear sense of his own preferences.

This course also provided the opportunity for students to learn what to expect from high school students. During a discussion of a writing assignment that students had been asked to do for the second day of class, the professor asked how it felt to work on the assignment. When students commented that the directions seemed overly structured, the professor responded, "But doing interviews is not all that easy for high school students, so some structure is probably necessary." He also commented on assumptions made about what high school students understand. "One of the hardest parts of the assignment for kids is understanding what a profile is. The assignment assumes that you know, which is not necessarily a good assumption." On the fourth day of class, students were given examples of student writing to which they were asked to respond. The papers had been written by junior high school remedial students. While serving as a springboard for a general discussion of issues related to grading, this assignment also provided the class with concrete examples of student writing that informed their developing expectations for students. One of their first assignments was to respond to a piece of student writing and suggest how they might help that student writer improve.

In addition to these concrete examples of student work, the professor provided glosses on appropriate assumptions and expectations for students. For example, in discussing their grading of student papers, the professor suggested that the class was "overly generous with . . . expectations for this group of students." During discussions of the writing process, the professor focused primarily on potential difficulties students face at each stage. This information helped shape the prospective teachers' understanding of what their students might find problematic about writing assignments.

The course also transmitted a whole repertoire of instructional strategies for teaching English. In addition to discussion about possible assignments and activities, the professor modeled a number of strategies in class. From the first day on, students worked in small groups, wrote in class, participated in group writing projects and peer-revision groups, kept learning logs, completed writing assignments, combined sentences, and read adolescent novels. Part of the professor's explicit goal for the course was to model activities he wanted to see students adopt in their own classrooms. "The course is fairly deliberately set up to involve them in the kinds of activities I'd like eventually to see them using in their classrooms and they may have less experience with. So there's an awful lot of group work; it's the basic mode of activity."

By the end of the course, students had lesson plans, unit plans, and copies of assignments for teaching writing, literature, and language, as well as a repertoire of possible strategies to use in their classrooms. Many of these activities surfaced in the classrooms of Vanessa, Steven, and Megan. All three teachers frequently used small-group work and assigned freewrites and journal writing; Steven used a modified version of "learning logs," as did Megan. Both Megan and Vanessa talked explicitly about going through their files from their curriculum and instruction courses for ideas and activities. In part, this experience with alternative activities and approaches to teaching English helped students overcome their own apprenticeships of observations as students in more traditional English classrooms.

Overcorrection: Overcoming the Apprenticeship of Observation

In addition to socializing students into the profession, the course helped students, both explicitly and implicitly, to overcome their tendency to rely on their memories of their own schooldays in shaping their classroom practice. On the very first day of class, students were encouraged to think back to their own experiences, while discussing the nature of English as a school subject. In this discussion, students referred to their own English teachers and the common subject matter and assignments they had encountered. Throughout the course, references to students' past experiences appeared in a variety of contexts, many of them elicited by the professor, such as his request for "old chestnuts" of English assignments.

By encouraging students to think back, however, the professor was not encouraging an easy, unreflective acceptance of past practice. Instead, he urged students to "rethink" the familiar, from the perspective of the theoretical frameworks they were developing in class. In a discussion of strategies to help high school students at different stages of the writing process, students suggested a number of familiar ideas; the professor commented on their place in the tradition of teaching English, while analyzing their adherence to the principles of writing instruction discussed in class. For example, when one student mentioned outlining as a strategy, the professor responded, "O.K. I always have mixed feelings about that. If you have them write an outline first and then write from it, people just don't write that way. . . . I prefer informal sorts of outlines, where they don't get locked into Roman numerals."

In the context of this discussion, the professor reminded students to "think differently about things you're very familiar with . . . there's a lot from the teachers' bag of tricks you can use . . . but you need to rethink them." By explicitly discussing strategies and assignments from the students' apprenticeships of observation, the professor also helped them to think more critically about the purposes, strengths, and weaknesses of these activities.

This course also used "overcorrection" as a strategy to overcome the power of students' prior experience in English classrooms. Examples of overcorrection appeared in a number of different contexts. The professor's decision to model primarily less traditional activities and assignments during class, represents one form of overcorrection for traditional practice. As he commented, overcoming instructional models students are familiar with from their own apprenticeships of observation is not a "trivial problem."

> One of the major problems with school right now is that almost all the writing students do is . . . essentially recitation. It tells back to the teacher what the teacher has already told the students. . . . It's also not a trivial problem to change. That's where most of the models are, in terms of most of the kinds of experiences the teachers have had themselves as writers in classrooms, have been that kind of writing. So we talk about ways to set up group activities around writing activities, in

providing editing groups and response groups, deferring grades until late in the grading period and basing it on a subset of work.

The implicit goal of the course attempted to replace one apprenticeship of observation with another. The use of less familiar activities in class ensured that the students, as prospective teachers, had recent hands-on experience with the strategies the professor would like them to use. While the prospective teachers encountered this new apprenticeship of observation in their role as students, they also analyzed the activities more critically from their role as teacher.

This overcorrection for traditional practice was apparent in students' responses to a writing assignment given to them as a model of instructional scaffolding. This particular assignment consisted of 13 steps involved in writing a descriptive paper. The professor outlined the assignment as follows:

> Cooper has built up a lesson with lots of scaffolding built in. There are activities to help [students] with different parts of the writing process. The one I had you read is a simplified version. On the board is a fleshed out version . . . there are thirteen steps spread out over six or seven class days . . . it takes a whole variety of different techniques and orchestrates them throughout the writing process. . . . It's not a boilerplate, since different things happen in different assignments.

The professor then asked students for their reactions to the assignment; most students felt the assignment was overly structured, allowing high school students little freedom to accomplish the assignment in their own way. Another student asked if high school students would still be "into" the assignment by the end of this process. The professor responded to this question by commenting, "My feeling is that it's overkill . . . but it's a good model to force you to think through what your alternatives are, instead of what we tend to do, which is to give them an assignment and have them write about it with too little apparatus."

After more discussion, the professor had the class practice by first generating "old chestnuts" of writing assignments and then working in groups to construct a similar multi-step assignment. The professor urged the class to "go ahead and overstructure. . . . By the end, we'll have seven or eight reasonably fleshed out writing assignments we can all take away with us."

The students' response to this task was almost formulaic; many of the completed assignments mimicked the original model, despite differences in the purposes for writing. One group developed a 15-step plan for teaching haiku. Their first comment as they began the task was to wonder, "How are we going to get 13 steps out of this?" In their plan, they incorporated many of what one participant termed "buzz words," such as revision, peer editing, generate, freewrite. Their self-consciousness in attempting the task reveals their unfamiliarity with both this genre of assignment and the technical vocabulary.[2] In the students' version of these assignments, which included a wide range of writing assignments from haiku to research papers, the average number of steps was 14.8; the same students who objected to the overstructure in the original assignment added an average of 1.8 steps to their own versions!

The inclusion of this model assignment and the requirement that students construct a similar one represents an instance of overcorrection. By asking students to emulate the 13-step example, the professor ensured that they would overstructure the activity they prepared. By providing an extreme example, something even he regarded as "overkill," he overcorrected for the traditional practice of providing assignments with very little structure beyond a paper topic, a practice students had encountered in their own apprenticeships of observation. The assignment gave students the chance to practice a new, and somewhat artificial, skill, which the professor hoped would later become a natural and implicit part of their pedagogical thinking. This overcorrection involved a process of moving from the unexamined and implicit aspects of the apprenticeship of observation to the artificial and explicit dimensions of an unfamiliar task and toward a goal of new routines.

Overcorrection for prior experience was also apparent in the effort to correct for the tendency to use memories of one's own abilities as a student to shape expectations for students. The student papers given to the class to respond to and correct represented fairly low levels of student ability; the first papers were written by students at the low end of both age—junior high—and ability—remedial class. The professor explicitly warned students against making too many assumptions about what high school students know. In their first response to actual student papers, when the prospective teachers assumed that the paragraphs were only part of larger papers, he told them they were "overly generous" in their expectations; the paragraph "*was* their [final] essay."

The emphasis on the needs and work of lower ability students surfaced in a number of ways. The course textbook on teaching writing described techniques developed with students from "difficult" classes. In response to a student question about the settings in which the authors worked, the professor replied, "The Kirby and Liner techniques pretty much got their start in

---

[2]While they used the words self-consciously and somewhat artificially at this stage, they were nonetheless beginning to develop a common vocabulary.

difficult classes. At the more academic level, kids do what the teachers tell them. In the lower stream, it's more obvious that things aren't working."

By providing both examples of student work and strategies for teaching that are oriented toward students of relatively low ability, the course forced the prospective teachers to break with their own experiences as successful students. In a class on teaching literature, the supervisor asked students to brainstorm titles of books they had "endured or enjoyed in high school or junior high school"; the supervisor then asked what percentage of the assigned books they actually read. When most students claimed to have read one hundred percent of the assigned books, the supervisor contrasted the prospective teachers' reading habits with a national survey done by the National Association of Educational Progress (NAEP).

> But we have a problem. You liked to read and read 80–100 percent of the assigned texts. . . . You liked reading so much you read in the bathtub. But listen to this. [reads aloud from NAEP survey] "Teenagers read very little for their own enjoyment. They watch more television and preferred movies to books. . . . About 10 percent of students couldn't read anything." That's a little food for thought.

By focusing on the disjunction between their own experiences as avid readers and the reading habits of typical teenagers, the course corrected for the tendency of prospective teachers to assume that their own interest in books was representative. The use of examples of student work that came almost solely from lower ability students sensitized prospective teachers to one extreme, the extreme with which they were probably less familiar. This overcorrection may help account for the lowered expectations for students found among the graduates of teacher education.

The Reflexive Class: Modeling Reasoned Practice

An important aspect of the instruction of this course involved its reflexive nature; just as the play *Hamlet* calls attention to the nature of language, so this class called attention to the nature of teaching. The course represented a common "case" of teaching available for analysis. From the first day, the professor called attention to his own teaching, modeling both a process of pedagogical reasoning and a critical stance toward teaching. On the first day of class, the professor commented on the poor example he had given by providing very little structure for the group assignment and making too many assumptions about students' ability to work in groups. On another day, after six groups of students had presented writing assignments to the rest of the class in a round-robin format, the professor asked, "Everyone still awake? That's not a particularly effective strategy for sharing. That's the tension of sharing. . . . I chose the wrong format. It isn't always necessary to share group work. This was an object lesson on the negative side."

His comments modeled a willingness to critique one's own teaching and to learn from mistakes. This reflexive process also pushed students out of the familiar role of student and into their newly chosen role of teacher; during the very first class, the professor told students "to switch heads" from student to teacher, as together they analyzed the group writing assignment from an explicitly pedagogical perspective. The professor described his purpose as "trying to make them much more self-conscious about things they've always taken for granted." The class critique of groupwork provided an explicit, collaborative rehearsal for a process of self-examination the professor hoped would become more automatic as the students gained experience. As the professor commented,

> The kind of process they're going through is explicit and not the least bit intuitive at first, because they don't have experience with it. It becomes much less routine and less awkward as they become less self-conscious about using it. And that should be happening. What they're internalizing should be automatic. And then, at a later stage, if they've internalized them, they should be available for that self-reflection. We're giving them a structure for stepping back, for being more self-critical.

The professor's reference to providing a structure to provoke and guide students' self-examinations suggests one of the ways in which the course functioned as a self-exemplification of the concept of instructional scaffolding. Explicit structures existed in the course to engage students in critiques of their own teaching. One of the assignments the professor used in the past was a final paper "requiring a critical analysis of themselves as teachers; it's a self-examination and it's a very difficult task." Prior to this self-analysis, however, the students had observed the professor critique his own teaching and participated in group discussions in which they were encouraged to critique their professor's instructional decisions. Students first rehearsed the skill of pedagogical reflection in a social setting. In an almost Vygotskyan image of the process of learning to teach, the professor hoped that the social rehearsal would help students internalize a "routine" of reflective practice.

This class was not the only arena in which students were given a chance to practice, in an interactive setting, the skills of reflection. In another course on the foundations of learning, students were required to interview each other about a lesson, observe the lesson, and then interview each other again after the observations. This assignment also provided an explicit structure for collegial reflection on teaching. The supervisory relationship built into the program of teacher education provided another opportunity for students to reflect on their teaching in the context of a collegial relationship. Other features of the larger teacher education program supported the learning occurring in the curriculum and instruction courses.

FEATURES OF THE TEACHER EDUCATION PROGRAM

The focus of this analysis on a single course should not minimize the importance of other aspects of the larger program of professional education. This curriculum and instruction sequence existed within a larger context, which included both other courses and an extended period of fieldwork. Features of this larger program necessarily contributed to the influence of the subject-specific component.

The teacher education program as a whole emphasized the subject-specific nature of secondary-school teaching. Subject-specific methods courses consisted of two-quarter sequences, and students were encouraged, and occasionally required, to take at least two electives in their content area. In English, all candidates enrolled in two quarters of curriculum and instruction in English; most chose to take an additional class in methods of teaching writing. At least nine units of a 45-unit program were devoted exclusively to the teaching of English. In addition to these nine units, teachers were encouraged to take two courses in the English or drama department, which added six more units to the subject-specific component of the program. At least half of the courses taken by students and one-third of the total number of units centered around the subject matter of English.

Other courses provided additional opportunities for discussions of subject-specific pedagogy. In seminars related to their field experiences, students spent an hour in general discussions and an additional hour in subject matter groups led by their supervisors. In other required courses, professors also broke students into subject matter groups for discussions of how the material related to their particular content areas. The larger structure and context of the program, then, supported the acquisition of pedagogical content knowledge through its emphasis on the subject-specific nature of secondary-school teaching.

The specific role played by supervisors in this program also reinforced the subject-specific courses in English. Supervisors of student teaching were graduate students with secondary teaching experience. University supervisors provide a potential link between coursework and fieldwork, as they commute between the worlds of the university and the school. In this program, the university supervisors also served as teaching assistants in the curriculum and instruction courses, providing an additional linkage between the course and the field. The professor commented on the important role played by the university supervisors.

> The supervisors work with me in many of the classes. We use what they're seeing in the classrooms to shape what we do in class, and vice versa. When it's working right, what goes on in class should be a sharpening of the practical kinds of things. . . . What we can do in class, which there is not time to do in supervision, includes the more systematic things like touching base with the literature, the more systematic frameworks, thinking through the "whys" and underlying purposes.

In their dual role as supervisors and as teaching assistants for the curriculum and instruction courses, supervisors played a major role in reinforcing the professor's philosophy in school settings and helping the students integrate the theoretical frameworks with classroom realities. In helping to select the English supervisors, the professor ensured that the supervisors shared his vision of teaching English, so that students did not receive contradictory messages.

The very nature of the fieldwork experiences also may have supported the influence of the curriculum and instruction classes. In this particular program, students worked as either student teachers or interns in local schools for two periods a day throughout the school year. Student teachers work in a master teacher's classroom; interns are responsible for their own classes. Megan, Steven, and Vanessa all worked as interns at public schools for their field experience. Internships provided them with the opportunity to practice, adapt, and refine the strategies suggested in their curriculum and instruction courses, without having to modify their approach to fit with that of a master teacher. In many ways, interns were best able to take advantage of the activities, lesson plans, and units presented in the curriculum and instruction classes, since they had more discretion about what to teach. Steven characterized his internship as a time to put his new ideas and philosophy into practice.

This distinction between student teaching and an internship may help to explain why the influence of teacher education was not "washed out" in the first year of teaching (Zeichner & Tabachnik, 1981). While student teachers must adapt what they learn in the university setting to the expectations and routines of a master teacher, interns were freer to try out new ideas in their classrooms. Because the central person responsible for the interns' supervision was the university supervisor, interns may have avoided the "two worlds pitfall" (Feiman-Nemser & Buchmann, 1985), in which students must negotiate between the differing norms of the university and the school site. Even though interns must conform to the external requirements of the department, school, and district, behind the classroom door they exercise more autonomy than student teachers.

Finally, the overall goals of the larger program of professional preparation supported the particular perspective being cultivated in the subject-specific courses. A common vision of both the teacher and the learner cut across the various components of this program of teacher education. According to its literature and staff, the program focused on preparing "reflective practitioners," teachers who are reflective about their teaching and the functions of schooling.[3] Teachers were viewed as professionals who make judgments on the basis of their professional knowledge and skill, not as implementers of "teacher-proof" curricula. Norms of professional collegiality also existed in the program as a whole; students were encouraged to see each other as resources in the process of learning to teach. As part of their course assignments, they were often asked to observe each other teach, to collaborate on assignments, and to share curriculum materials. The emphasis in the curriculum and instruction class on "principled practice" and on collegiality was mirrored by the emphasis of the program as a whole.

The program also offered a fairly consistent view of learning as the active construction of knowledge. The view of the student as language learner, presented in the curriculum and instruction course, emphasized learning as a developmental process, in which students experiment with language while developing their own implicit theories of how language works; the student reader also constructs a personal meaning from literature. From this perspective, the role of the teacher is to bridge between the students' prior experience and the content to be studied. Prospective teachers encountered a very similar perspective toward teaching and learning in their required course on the foundations of learning.

This consistency in visions of teaching and learning may make the traditionally weak intervention of teacher education much more powerful, since what students learn in one course is reinforced in another. In fact, the ideas encountered in curriculum and instruction began to function as a filter for what students reported learning in other courses.

All three teachers in this sample reported that their responses to other professional courses were shaped, in part, by their participation in their curriculum and instruction courses. Steven, for example, reported adopting a general theory of education from his foundations class that best fit the conceptual frameworks being developed in his curriculum and instruction course: "I think it was Roger's *Freedom to Learn* especially that struck me as an interesting approach and also that tied in rather nicely with [the English

---

[3]One indication of the students' awareness of the goal of reflective practice appeared during a recent graduation, in which the graduates of the teacher education program covered their caps with aluminum foil so that they would be, literally, reflective.

education professor's] ideas." Megan rejected the ideas in one course, which she felt offered an approach to language instruction that contradicted the conceptual frameworks developed in her curriculum and instruction course.

> As far as English goes, some things were helpful, thinking about how kids acquire language and how I could help that. But [the course] contradicted a lot of stuff we had talked about in C & I, and I had practiced what we'd done in C & I and seen that it was a good thing to do and I respected the professor, and I believed in that program by then, and this was antithetical.

Vanessa reported that she found a course on groupwork less helpful than some of her other courses only because she had had extensive exposure to groupwork through her subject-specific courses and her supervisors.

> And the English section had been doing groupwork and had put a lot of weight on groupwork since English C & I and the supervisors and everybody, and I'd read a lot of stuff about it. So if I had not . . . been exposed to it, [the class] would have been very helpful for that, but I didn't learn that much that I didn't already know.

Vanessa's comment illustrates the "conceptual redundancy" that existed among the various courses in this program of teacher education, as similar images of teaching and learning processes cut across courses and supervision. This conceptual coherence, experienced by the prospective teachers as redundancy, may also have contributed to the influence of both the program and its subject-specific component.

CONCLUSION

In analyzing the features of the curriculum and instruction sequence in English that influenced the development of pedagogical content knowledge by Steven, Megan, and Vanessa, it may be helpful to put this course into a larger context by looking at other frameworks that try to define "effective" programs of teacher education. Griffin (1986) analyzed the features of effective clinical teacher education and identified seven critical features, five of which would apply to both the subject-specific coursework and the larger program of teacher education described in this chapter. The five features include a well-articulated purpose, participation and collaboration, a theoretical knowledge base, a developmental progression, and an analytical and reflective perspective toward practice.

A second framework, developed as part of the National Center for Research on Teacher Education (Cohen, 1986), proposes three features related to the academic quality of teacher education programs. Posed as dichotomies, these features contrast: the portrayal of knowledge as fixed versus knowledge as evolving and tentative; teacher education students as passive vessels versus students as active constructors of knowledge; and instruction as transmission of knowledge versus instruction through discourse. In the curriculum and instruction courses, knowledge was seen as incomplete, students actively constructed their evolving knowledge of teaching, and instruction proceeded through discussion and dialogue.

A third framework, developed by Katz and Raths (1988), also poses dichotomies, which are labeled as persistent dilemmas in teacher education. Arguing that the solutions to each dilemma are mutually exclusive, the authors suggest that how a teacher education program resolves these dilemmas will contribute to its impact on students as well as the students' satisfaction with the program. The dilemmas include: whether to aim for coverage or breadth of content or to focus on mastery or depth; whether to offer eclectic programs or thematic programs; an emphasis on current needs of students versus an emphasis on future needs; an evaluative stance toward students versus a supportive stance; whether to teach toward current school practices or to encourage innovative practices; and whether to assess students globally or specifically. The subject-specific component of this program resolved these dilemmas in favor of mastery of a few key concepts; a thematic approach; a supportive relationship among supervisors, professor, and students; and a decision to encourage innovative practice. While clearly stating that the courses were designed to meet students' current needs, in fact the course served both current and future needs.

A final framework for thinking about the influence of the curriculum and instruction course is the very framework advocated by the course for the teaching of English—instructional scaffolding. The five features of instructional scaffolding (Langer & Applebee, 1986)—including ownership, appropriateness, support, collaboration, and transfer of control—could be used to describe the nature of instruction in this class. Within the course itself, students were encouraged to develop their own ideas and materials and to feel ownership for the perspectives being developed in class through the use of learning logs, writing assignments, and other tasks. The content of the course consciously addressed the needs of students at different points during their program and distinguished between knowledge necessary for teachers and knowledge necessary for researchers, thus meeting the criterion of appropriateness. The structure of the course provided a great deal of support for students as they learned to teach. Students first developed lessons and assignments in groups, with explicit models and guidelines, tasks they would later have to do on their own. The relationship between professor and students was a collaborative one; on the first day of class, the issue of grading was defined, essentially, as a non-issue. The purpose of the class, and of the relationship between professor and students, was to help students learn to teach.

These four different frameworks converge around four common principles for teacher education. All of the frameworks suggest the importance of students' active construction of knowledge through collaborative relationships with professors, supervisors, and master teachers. When students actively participate in the construction of their knowledge about teaching, they are more likely to feel a sense of ownership for the ideas and perspectives developed during professional preparation. As Griffin (1986) suggests,

> Collaboration is related to ownership. The teacher who has had some hand in formulating and carrying forward the effort (as opposed to being only the recipient of a set of externally-imposed specifications) will very probably feel a strong investment in bringing it to successful operation. (p. 12)

Students who feel ownership for the ideas and knowledge acquired during teacher education, as Megan, Steven, and Vanessa did, may be more likely to implement the perspectives developed during their programs. Inherent in this general principle is a view of knowledge that, as Cohen (1986) suggests, is tentative and flexible.

Knowledge that helps prospective teachers develop a sense of the overarching purposes for teaching subject matter and the strategies that are consistent with those larger purposes may be more influential in the long run than specific prescriptions for practice. An understanding of the theoretical principles and research that underlie a particular perspective toward practice can help beginning teachers justify and defend their choices, particularly when those pedagogical choices run counter to standard practice (Lamme & Ross, 1981; McCaleb, 1979). This theoretical knowledge can also shape what teachers learn from their classroom experience, as Griffin (1986) suggests.

> Theory is particularly powerful in helping prospective and career teachers understand and make sense of their professional worlds. Theoretical formulations suggest and define connections between disparate pieces of the complex teaching and schooling puzzle, and thus lead thoughtful teachers to make their own discoveries as a consequence of increased understandings. They can also provide a body of shared understanding across groups of teachers who are trying to come to decisions about how to proceed in teaching. (p. 14)

Because teachers will need to apply the general knowledge acquired during professional preparation in specific situations, they also need to understand how to adapt theoretical knowledge to the demands of particular students and schools. By engaging students in hands-on activities and allowing them to explore the connections between theoretical knowledge and classroom practices, this curriculum and instruction class helped students make the connection between theory and practice.

All of the frameworks also stress the importance of support for prospective teachers. This analysis suggests that support may involve explicit overcorrection for prior experiences and assumptions prospective teachers have developed during their apprenticeships of observation. Teacher education must help students break with their prior experience as students and begin to develop the perspective of a teacher (Feiman-Nemser & Buchmann, 1985). As the prospective teachers are still students in teacher education classrooms, this process can be tricky.[4] Helping prospective teachers balance their simultaneous roles as students of teaching and teachers of students is one of the challenges for teacher educators. Involving prospective teachers in forms of guided practice is another feature of support. This guided practice may move from overly structured, explicit, and interactive rehearsals of the processes and strategies that will later become more tacit routines of teaching. Planning may be one example of a process that must first be explicit before it can become routinized. As cooperating teachers have already mastered many of these routines, their knowledge may be relatively tacit. One role for teacher educators, then, is to make this tacit knowledge explicit for prospective teachers and to help them develop a process of pedagogical thinking that, while artificial at first, will later become second nature.

Inherent in the concept of support is the criterion of appropriateness. In order for prospective teachers to participate in the processes of constructing knowledge and practicing new routines, they must perceive the usefulness of such activities. This criterion can result in a recurrent tension between theory and practice. As prospective teachers enter student teaching situations, they are likely to be more receptive to strategies and techniques they can use immediately in their classroom; they may be less receptive, however, to the theoretical underpinnings of these strategies. The curriculum of teacher education, then, must balance both the current and future needs of teachers in determining appropriateness, relying on what Griffin (1986) termed "a developmental progression."

Finally, both the frameworks discussed above and this analysis suggest the importance of a coherent and consistent vision of teaching and learning, what Griffin (1986) terms purpose and Katz and Raths (1988) call thematic. Programs that feature explicit visions of the nature of teaching and learning may be more powerful interventions than programs that lack this conceptual

---

[4]The role confusion is apparent even in the language used to discuss students of teacher education. They are variously referred to as students, prospective teachers, postulant teachers, and student teachers.

coherence. This feature may help explain the impact of "thematic" programs of teacher education, which are organized around a particular theme (Barnes, 1987) and offer versions of required courses that are consistent with the theme of the larger program. The program from which Steven, Megan, and Vanessa graduated had a general vision both of learning as the active construction of knowledge and of teaching as a reflective, intentional, and intellectual endeavor, in which teachers plan instruction around the prior knowledge and beliefs of the students and the features of the particular subject matter to be taught. The specific curriculum and instruction course offered a more elaborated view, consistent with the more general conceptions, of the purposes for teaching English and the nature of learning to write and read literature.

Four general features, then, seemed to contribute to the influence of this particular curriculum and instruction course: a coherent vision of teaching and learning, organized around the specific subject matter to be taught; a collaborative relationship among professor, supervisors, and students, in which the prospective teachers helped construct their evolving knowledge concerning the teaching of English for which they could feel a sense of ownership; the existence of necessary support, or "scaffolding" for prospective teachers as they acquired the skills and pedagogical perspective for teaching and developed a reflective stance toward practice; and a developmental perspective on learning to teach, in which the curriculum provided the knowledge and skills appropriate for both the current and future needs and concerns of prospective teachers. One avenue for future research in teacher education involves further investigation and explorations of these features across a variety of teacher preparation programs.

6

Images of the Possible

As Hamlet so aptly observed, "there is nothing either good or bad, but thinking makes it so." How we think about the purposes of education, and the purposes for teaching English in particular, will necessarily color our readings of these cases of beginning teachers. Some may argue that the higher expectations embedded in the curricular choices of the teachers without teacher education are exactly what we need more of in our schools. While Ravitch and Finn (1987) may deplore the selection of adolescent literature among the graduates of teacher education and applaud the canonical choices of Lance, others will argue just the opposite. What is less debatable is the extent to which subject-specific teacher education coursework influenced how Megan, Steven, and Vanessa thought about and taught English.

The contrasts between these two groups of teachers help us understand more about the relationship between professional education and professional knowledge, specifically the role of subject-specific coursework in the development of pedagogical content knowledge. Studying teachers who have entered teaching without teacher education also provides another way to investigate the process of learning to teach. Contrasting teachers with and without teacher education can highlight taken-for-granted assumptions about learning from experience. As policy makers legislate a variety of new structures for entry into teaching, researchers can take advantage of these natural experiments to study the relationship between alternative forms of teacher preparation and their influence on the development of teachers' knowledge and beliefs about teaching (Ball, 1990; Gomez, 1990; Natriello, Zumwalt, Hansen, & Frisch, 1988; Rorro, 1987).

IMPLICATIONS FOR ALTERNATE ROUTES INTO TEACHING

In efforts to increase the numbers of talented college graduates who enter teaching, legislators in different states have developed a number of alternate routes into teaching, many of which bypass traditional university-based teacher preparation. In many instances, beginning teachers in alternative programs take professional courses in generic pedagogical knowledge and skills at the same time they are teaching in classrooms. The implicit assumption of these programs suggests that teachers can rely on their knowledge of content in learning to teach; the rest will come through a smattering of generic pedagogical principles, classroom experience, and perhaps mentoring. Well-educated and knowledgeable about their subject, Kate, Jake, and Lance would all fit the image of the kind of teacher policy makers would like to lure into teaching. Their experiences in their first year of teaching, as well as the experiences of a number of teaching interns in one alternate route program (Shulman, 1989), suggest some troublesome implications of the assumption that subject matter knowledge and classroom experience can suffice as teacher education.

Although much pedagogical knowledge has been characterized as common sense, knowledge is not hanging, ripe and fully formed, in the classroom, waiting to be plucked by inexperienced teachers. Planning for instruction and subsequent student learning might serve as an example of common sense concerning teaching, yet neither Kate, Jake, and Lance, nor a number of interns in an alternate route program (Shulman, 1989), found it easy to rethink their subject matter in terms of what students might learn. Shulman (1989) concluded, "These teachers had no prior conception of how to develop a unit that included appropriate instruction for their students" (p. 6). Learning from experience requires that teachers first interpret classroom events in ways that make sense to them. Without frameworks for understanding teaching and learning, how beginning teachers without professional preparation interpret experience may prove problematic.

As others have argued, learning from experience alone can be miseducative (Dewey, 1904; Feiman-Nemser & Buchmann, 1985). Classroom experience by itself taught Jake that students' difficulties with Shakespeare resulted from their lack of ability and motivation. In contrast, concepts such as "instructional scaffolding" helped graduates of teacher education to create bridges and appropriate support and structures for students as they encounter unfamiliar and difficult content.

Lack of formal professional preparation may also reinforce the pervasive belief that there is little to learn about teaching, a belief that helped lead to many alternate route policies in the first place. Jake, Lance, and, to a lesser extent, Kate all assumed that experience in the classroom would teach them what they needed to know. Jake decided that teaching required little more than the ability to act or to sell a product, while Lance rejected what he termed "the psychology of teaching." An evaluation of New Jersey's alternative route program (Rodman, 1988) found that the beginning teachers wanted less, not more, training for teaching, a finding that may imply that the beginning teachers believed there was little to learn about teaching outside of direct classroom experience. A preliminary study of seven alternate route programs (Adelman, 1986) concluded, "In essence, participants confirmed their belief in the age old adage that 'you learn to teach by teaching'" (p. 37). If their very entry into the profession reinforces the importance of direct experience and the relative unimportance of more systematic knowledge about teaching, how will these teachers respond to opportunities for continuing staff development?

This faith in the value of personal experience may also prevent beginning teachers from enlisting the help of more experienced colleagues. If beginning teachers who enter teaching without formal teacher education both feel that there is little to learn about teaching and do not see colleagues as potential resources, they are unlikely to take advantage of the services of mentor teachers, even when they are provided (Shulman, 1989). If the nature of schools as workplaces hinders the development of norms of collegiality (Little, 1982; Lortie, 1975), beginning teachers are unlikely to develop these norms on their own in schools. If beginning teachers are to value other teachers as colleagues, then their professional preparation, whether in alternate route programs or in traditional programs, must model these norms and structure opportunities for teachers to work and learn together.

The most serious implication these teachers' experiences pose for alternative route programs, however, concerns the teachers' emerging beliefs about students. If people are attracted to teaching by their expectations of teaching students more or less like themselves—the presumption of shared identity Jackson (1986) discusses—or of dealing with the subject matter in ways that will be intellectually challenging for themselves, they may presume a fairly elite group of potential students. As new teachers, however, they are unlikely to encounter these elite students. Without help, teachers may learn to blame the students for not learning, as Jake did, rather than to rethink their own assumptions about a teacher's responsibility to teach a wide range of students. This potential mismatch between teachers' implicit assumptions about students and the realities of their own students' abilities and interests may lead not only to instances of mislearning but to quick disenchantment with teaching.

Without recourse to more systematic knowledge about teaching that might help them develop more effective classroom strategies, and with little belief in the value of learning from colleagues, beginning teachers can become frustrated and overwhelmed by the difficulties of teaching. Lance left teaching precipitously after his resignation from his internship experience, while Jake left after his second year.

PROFESSIONAL KNOWLEDGE AND PROFESSIONAL EDUCATION

All prospective secondary teachers face the task of rethinking their subject matter from a more pedagogical perspective. Studying literature in college seminars and teaching English in high school classrooms are clearly not isomorphic activities. This transition to pedagogical thinking, however, is not automatic (Feiman-Nemser & Buchmann, 1985). While pedagogical understandings of content derive partly from disciplinary knowledge, teachers also need explicit knowledge about the purposes and strategies involved in teaching particular subject matter in secondary schools as well as knowledge about how students learn specific content.

Disciplinary knowledge alone, while crucial for teaching, does not provide teachers with the pedagogical understanding necessary for teaching a wide range of students (Wilson, 1988). Understanding *Hamlet* well is not the same as understanding how to engage high school students in the play; the latter requires knowledge of how students approach literature in the context of school and knowledge of the purposes for teaching literature in secondary school, as well as a repertoire of instructional strategies. Creating appropriate pedagogical representations of the content requires that teachers have sufficient understanding of how students learn particular subjects (McDiarmid, Ball, & Anderson, 1989).

As we prepare teachers to work in secondary schools, we need to consider both the content knowledge they bring with them to professional preparation and the pedagogical content knowledge they will need for teaching. Teacher education courses can provide a context for the re-examination of subject matter from a purposefully pedagogical perspective and help prospective teachers develop sound conceptions of what it means to teach their subject matter to diverse students. While prospective teachers can learn much from their field experiences, they do not seem to develop new conceptions of teaching their subject matter from classroom experience alone. Although they may learn that strategies they remember from college courses do not translate well into classroom practice, prospective and beginning teachers may find it difficult to reconceptualize on their own their purposes for teaching their subjects.

Subject-specific teacher education coursework can help teachers construct conceptions of what it means to teach a subject, conceptions grounded in current knowledge about teaching and learning specific content areas in secondary school. Prospective teachers can explore the pedagogical implications of different conceptions, connecting these conceptions with broader issues such as equity and access to knowledge. As methods courses by nature are inherently practical, exploring more theoretical issues in this context can provide students with the opportunity to reflect on classroom practices from a broader perspective. Prospective teachers may be unlikely to make these connections between the practical and theoretical on their own. Accordingly, teacher educators must help create this tension between the practical and theoretical by incorporating both into their courses; as teacher educators, we too must construct bridges for our students. Away from the press of high school classrooms, university courses can take advantage of that distance to encourage reflection that explores the theoretical foundations and pedagogical and social implications of particular practices (Richert, in press). For the theoretical to be compelling for prospective teachers, however, it must be linked to the practical realities of classroom teaching.

In addition to conceptions of what it means to teach particular subjects, subject-specific teacher education can contribute to prospective teachers' understanding of what secondary-school students understand and misunderstand about specific topics. Research on learning has begun to focus on student misconceptions in science, as well as the informal strategies students use in solving mathematics problems. Research on writing has uncovered the various processes in which student writers engage and the ways in which these processes might differ for experienced writers. New work in history investigates the ways in which high school students and historians read and understand historical documents (Wineburg, 1990).

The findings of such research can prove invaluable to prospective teachers, when they are linked to implications for instructional practice. This kind of knowledge of student understanding in a content area can help teachers make sense of student difficulties and think of instructional solutions within the context of a theoretical understanding of how students learn particular topics. As prospective teachers report learning about student difficulties through classroom experiences, field experiences could be organized to take advantage of this opportunity for learning; the reasons for student difficulties and misconceptions and strategies for helping students could then be explored in the context of subject-specific methods courses. Prospective teachers might be asked to interview and work with high school students on particular topics that research has shown to be problematic. Bringing these concrete examples of student difficulties into their subject-specific courses can help prospective teachers learn more about student understanding within a subject area, while again bridging the worlds of the school and university. A theoretical understanding of the various sources of teacher knowledge can help us exploit the potential of the different contexts within teacher education programs for supporting different kinds of student learning. In linking field experiences to courses, we can take advantage of the distinct opportunities for learning presented by each (Dewey, 1904; Feiman-Nemser, 1983).

Teacher education also encompasses the courses taken in arts and sciences. As undergraduates, prospective teachers develop not only knowledge about the content they will later teach, but ideas about how to teach that content. The ways in which these beginning teachers all drew upon their college courses as sources of ideas about teaching illustrates the role of arts and science faculty as de facto teacher educators. Jake's professor may not have realized that in addition to teaching Jake to write, she was also teaching him a model of teaching writing, just as Kate's professor might be surprised to learn that he taught Kate about how to teach a text. Past work on teachers has emphasized the importance of the apprenticeships of observation in elementary and secondary schools (Lortie, 1975). This study suggests that we pay closer attention to what prospective teachers learn in college about the pedagogy connected with particular topics and subject areas.

As experiences in college classrooms are more recent and therefore more available (Tversky & Kahnemann, 1974), perhaps it is not so surprising that prospective teachers draw heavily from their undergraduate courses in preparing to teach their subjects. This influence may be particularly strong for secondary-school teachers, as both their preparation and prospective careers are organized around the subject matters they study in college. Yet as virtually all these six teachers found, the pedagogical methods they encountered in their college courses did not translate well into secondary-school classrooms.

This is not to suggest that we necessarily teach undergraduates as we would have teachers teach high school students (although in some instances it might improve college pedagogy). However, teacher education must directly confront the assumptions about subject-specific pedagogy developed during the undergraduate portion of teacher education. Again, field experiences could be integrated into these explorations of the different purposes and methods of secondary school and college teaching. Prospective teachers could be asked to observe middle school, high school, and college teachers teach the same content—for example, a Shakespeare play or *Huckleberry Finn* in English, or the American Revolution in history. In their subject-specific methods classes they could then explore the different pedagogical treatments the same content received in different contexts and how to make sense of those differences from an explicitly pedagogical perspective.

These recommendations for countering the lessons of the apprenticeship of observation all assume a closer link between teacher education coursework and field experiences than is typical of the teacher education curriculum (Edmundson, 1989). Part of the movement toward professional development centers focuses on the promise of this integration of fieldwork and coursework. As researchers have found, we have much to learn from the wisdom of experienced practitioners regarding pedagogical content knowledge (Wilson, 1988; Wineburg & Wilson, in press). With greater cooperation between professional development schools and universities, we hope to repair the pitfalls that line the commute between these two very different institutions (Feiman-Nemser & Buchmann, 1985).

Academic departments in colleges and universities must take their roles in the preparation of teachers more seriously, just as teacher education must consider issues related to subject matter. Researchers are beginning to investigate what undergraduates, both prospective teachers and others, learn about the nature of history and about teaching history from their undergraduate coursework (McDiarmid, 1989). The Presidents' Forum on Teaching as a Profession is also engaging universities in the process of examining their role in the recruitment and education of teachers. The lesson of pedagogical content knowledge is not one of division but of union; just as content and pedagogy are inextricably linked in teaching, so are arts and sciences and education faculties inevitably united in the preparation of teachers.

POLICY AND PROMISE IN TEACHER EDUCATION

While this study illustrates the potential linkage between pedagogical content knowledge and subject-specific pedagogical coursework, we need further research on the ways in which different facets of professional preparation contribute to the development of knowledge, beliefs, and classroom practice among prospective teachers. In this instance, subject-specific methods courses proved to be a powerful source of pedagogical content knowledge for Megan, Steven, and Vanessa. Yet, as N. L. Gage (1978) is fond of reminding us, case studies can prove only that something is possible, not that it is probable. Yet invoking possibility itself can be a virtue.

> One major virtue of a case study is its ability to evoke images of the possible. . . . It is often the goal of policy to pursue the possible, not only to support the probable or frequent. The well-crafted case instantiates the possible, not only documenting that it can be done, but also laying out at least one detailed example of how it was organized, developed, and pursued. (Shulman, 1983, p. 495)

These case studies suggest an "image of the possible" in teacher education—an instance in which subject-specific coursework did influence beginning teachers' beliefs and practice—rather than a portrait of the probable. These cases, however, are necessarily bound by the nature of both the context and the individuals who participated. In other methods courses, the content and instruction may differ radically. A recent study of the curriculum of teacher education programs (Edmundson, 1989) suggests that the courses I describe would be considered anomalies in the world of teacher education.

One challenge for teacher educators, however, is to strive toward the possible rather than the probable. In this time of flux in teacher education policies, teacher educators can counter the movement toward waiving and limiting pedagogical coursework not by arguing for the commonplace but by creating exemplary programs and courses and investigating their effects on prospective teachers. This case provides both the specific details and more general frameworks to consider in developing such courses. As Zeichner (1988) argues,

> The important thing at this point in time is to begin efforts to build a base of more valid information about courses and programs that will be able to inform those who make teacher education policy as well as those who teach and work in the courses and programs. (p. 25)

Case studies of a variety of different teacher education programs, such as the ones conducted by the Study of the Education of Educators (Goodlad, 1988) and the National Center for Research on Teacher Education (Feiman-Nemser, 1987) can help provide the analyses necessary to build a richer conceptualization of the teacher education curriculum and its influence on how prospective teachers learn to teach.

With widespread predictions of coming teacher shortages, we face a crisis in teacher education. The temptation to take shortcuts in preparing teachers will only increase. Developing routes into teaching, whether expedient shortcuts or in-depth programs, demands a deeper theoretical understanding of teacher knowledge and its sources. Lacking such knowledge, we will be hard pressed to refute the persistent and pervasive beliefs that teacher education coursework is, at best, irrelevant and that classroom experience alone can serve as teacher education.

APPENDIX A

Methodology

As I suspect is true of many research projects, my interest in the effects of teacher education has its roots in personal biography. Having acquired a degree in English and a teaching credential during the teacher glut of the 1970s, I could not find a public school teaching job. Determined to teach, I taught in government programs and at independent schools, where teacher education is neither required nor particularly valued. An excellent background in one's subject matter, plus an interest in teaching, serve as adequate preparation for teaching in many independent schools. Throughout my years of secondary-school teaching, I wondered what difference, if any, teacher education might have made to the bright, well-educated teachers with whom I worked.

My interest in pedagogical content knowledge emerged from my experiences working with Lee Shulman of Stanford University on a research project entitled "Knowledge Growth in a Profession," funded by the Spencer Foundation. This research focused particularly on the role of subject matter knowledge in learning to teach. How did beginning secondary-school teachers use their prior subject matter knowledge in planning for instruction? What did these beginning teachers learn about their content areas as they learned more about teaching? Out of this research grew the concept of pedagogical content knowledge (Shulman, 1986a), the knowledge necessary for teaching specific school subjects.

While one of the initial purposes of the knowledge growth study was to investigate the role that teacher education played in the growth and transformation of beginning teachers' subject matter knowledge, time and resources precluded a careful study of the issues related to professional preparation. However, we recognized that this was a missing piece of the research, a realization prodded by thoughtful critiques of our work provided by Sharon Feiman-Nemser and Karen Zumwalt, among others.

Both the research questions and aspects of the research design and methods grew out of my participation with this research project. The logical link between subject-specific coursework and pedagogical content knowledge allowed me to investigate further ideas about the potential influence of professional coursework. I also developed ideas about the use of case study research during my participation with the knowledge growth research team. In order to portray as fully as possible the knowledge the beginning teachers possessed as they entered teaching and the growth and transformation of this knowledge during teaching, we used a variety of structured and semi-structured interviews, subject-specific tasks and card sorts, and classroom observations, which resulted in extensive case studies of each teacher (e.g., Grossman, 1987). These lengthy case studies were the result of a great deal of discussion and debate about the nature, purpose, and structure of a case study designed to contribute to theoretical understanding. My participation in this project helped provide a repertoire of research strategies with which to study teacher knowledge, as well as a specific focus for my more general interest in the acquisition of knowledge and skill during teacher preparation.

CASE STUDY DESIGN

This study used a case study methodology, as its purpose was to generalize to a theoretical framework about teacher knowledge and its possible sources. As Yin (1984) suggests, "Case studies . . . are generalizable to theoretical propositions and not to populations or universes . . . and the investigator's goal is to expand and generalize theories" (p. 21). The case study approach to research on teacher knowledge represents an attempt to gather in-depth data on the content, character, and organization of an individual's knowledge for the purposes of contributing to a broader conceptualization of teacher knowledge and its use in teaching (Grossman & Wilson, 1987).

To call something "case study research," however, says more about the nature of the unit of analysis than about any particular strategies of data collection. Each individual case becomes the first unit of analysis, as the researcher identifies patterns and themes within the individual case that can be useful in the cross-case analysis. Case study research can draw on a wide variety of data collection strategies; the common thread of case study research is the identification, conceptualization, and elaboration of an individual case, while setting the particular case within a larger theoretical and naturalistic context.

The design of this study encompasses multiple case studies of six first-year English teachers, three of whom had graduated from the same program of teacher preparation and three of whom entered teaching without formal training. My decision to include only graduates of the same teacher education program reflects the difficulties in documenting teachers' attributions of knowledge acquisition. By looking at three graduates of the same program, and by observing the subject-specific coursework offered by the program, I increased the chances of finding patterns of influence among the graduates and mapping the acquisition of pedagogical content knowledge back to professional coursework. Much of the research done on the influence of teacher education coursework has relied on retrospective, self-reports of teachers, most of whom report little influence from teacher education. While one explanation, and the one generally accepted, suggests that professional coursework is at best a weak intervention, a second explanation might be that researchers did not probe for the potential contribution of coursework beyond the initial and consistent finding that teachers attribute most of their knowledge acquisition to student teaching (Lanier & Little, 1986; Lortie, 1975). By maximizing the contrasts between the two groups of teachers, the design of this study also maximized the possibility of identifying patterns of influence resulting from professional preparation.

INFORMANTS

The informants for this study were six first-year English teachers in the San Francisco Bay Area. In many ways, these teachers represent an elite group of beginning teachers (Kerr, 1983; Schlechty & Vance, 1983). As I wanted to control for subject matter knowledge in this study, I tried to find informants with strong backgrounds in English. Jake and Steven graduated with degrees in English from elite colleges, while Megan and Kate both studied comparative literature at prestigious research universities. Lance was completing his doctorate in comparative literature at the time of the study. Vanessa, the only teacher without an undergraduate major in literature, switched out of an English major to study journalism in college. These six teachers fall into two general groups: Lance, Jake, and Kate all entered teaching without formal professional preparation, while Megan, Steven, and Vanessa all graduated from the same fifth-year program of teacher education.

While I had hoped to control for teaching context in this study, I found I was unable to locate sufficient informants exclusively in either public schools or private schools. As a result, two of the three teachers with teacher education, Megan and Steven, taught in suburban, multi-racial public high schools, while only one of the teachers without teacher education, Lance, taught in a public school; to complicate matters further, he resigned from his job before I could observe him teach. The other two teachers without teacher education, Jake and Kate, both taught at independent schools, as did Vanessa. Jake and Vanessa taught at the same all-boys independent school, which provided the opportunity for at least one cross-case analysis in which teaching context was controlled. Again, the case study approach allowed me to make sense of an individual teacher's data with reference to the particular context in which he or she worked. Nonetheless, the differences in teaching context proved to be an important variable to consider in the interpretation of the data for this study, as teaching context and type of preparation are confounded.

One potential threat to the validity of the study arises from the central contrast between these two groups of teachers. While I tried to control, successfully, for subject matter knowledge and, unsuccessfully, for teaching context, I could not control for the effects of teachers' self-selection into or out of professional preparation. Teachers who choose to enter professional preparation may simply be different from teachers who choose to forgo formal teacher education. Certainly, a difference in commitment to the profession of teaching seemed to exist between the two groups in this study. However, as this study was conducted after the graduates had completed their professional preparation, it is difficult to know if the difference in commitment resulted from their professional education or if it existed prior to teacher education. In some sense, Steven's case demonstrates that he entered teacher education only after making the decision that he enjoyed teaching; his internship experience was a way to test the waters. The differences between the two groups are still of significance to policy makers, however, as teachers recruited into alternative routes to teaching have also made a de facto decision to forgo traditional preparation.

A second issue related to the potential validity of this study concerns the intellectual ability of the teachers themselves. When compared with studies of the general intellectual ability of people who enter teaching (Kerr, 1983; Schlechty & Vance, 1983; Vance & Schlechty, 1982), the teachers in this study are clearly atypical. This disjunction would be disturbing if my purpose were to generalize my results to teachers in general. As my purpose is to generalize to theory, however, the atypicality of the teachers becomes theoretically advantageous. By selecting teachers who were all bright and well-prepared in their subject matter and then choosing graduates of a demanding and prestigious program of teacher education, this study may offer a clearer vision of what, if anything, teacher education can contribute to the process of learning to teach.

DATA COLLECTION

Data collection for the case studies included both interviews and classroom observation. The interviews were structured to elicit information on the pedagogical content knowledge of the beginning teachers and its sources. As knowledge is an intangible and elusive object of study, the interviews represented different approaches to eliciting these data. While some of the interviews asked informants directly about their beliefs and knowledge about the teaching of English, other interviews included tasks that would theoretically require teachers to draw upon their pedagogical content knowledge; during these interviews, both the teachers' decisions and their rationales for the decisions served as indicators of their underlying knowledge and beliefs. The different types of interviews, along with the classroom observations, provided the opportunity to look for both explicit and implicit knowledge the teachers drew upon during interviews, tasks, and classroom practice.

Another potential threat to the validity of this study concerns the very nature of these interviews. In some cases, the questions asked of the teachers may have prompted them to reflect on topics they had not previously considered; for example, asking teachers about their goals for students may have prompted them to construct these goals extemporaneously. In this sense, the interviews may have provoked the construction of new knowledge, in addition to eliciting already existing knowledge. Given the interactive nature of this research and the dynamic nature of knowledge, I needed to take this possibility into consideration as I analyzed the data, partly by looking across different types of data for evidence of teachers' knowledge.

The first interview was designed to collect data on the teachers' conceptions of teaching English, including their beliefs and knowledge about the purposes for teaching secondary-school English. The second interview involved a card-sort task, in which the teachers sorted the courses they had taken in college and graduate school according to how the courses had influenced their knowledge and conceptions of English and their knowledge and conceptions of teaching English. In addition, at the end of the interview, the graduates of teacher education were given just the titles of their teacher education courses, which included their fieldwork experience, to sort and discuss. The card-sort served as a stimulus for discussions both about the teachers' pedagogical content knowledge, particularly their conceptions of teaching English and their knowledge of instructional strategies, and about the sources of their ideas and beliefs. The way in which the teachers approached the task also provided data on the relationship between their knowledge of English and their knowledge of teaching English; one teacher, for example, did not resort the cards according to how they influenced his ideas about teaching English, claiming that how he thought about English was the same as how he thought about teaching English.

The third and fourth interviews involved specific tasks, which were designed to elicit further data on the teachers' pedagogical content knowledge. The third interview asked teachers to read a brief but dense poem, "The Death of the Ball Turret Gunner" by Randall Jarrell. Following a discussion of the poem itself, teachers were asked to think about teaching the poem. The interview probed for knowledge of student understanding, curricular knowledge, and conceptions of teaching poetry. Additional probes for the interview asked teachers for the reasons underlying their decisions and possible sources for their ideas. This interview also included a brief period of simulated interactive teaching, in which I adopted the role of a student who was having tremendous difficulty understanding the poem and asked questions of the teachers; they were asked to respond to me as they would to an actual student.

The fourth interview involved simulated planning for three hypothetical courses: a general-track freshman English class; an eleventh-grade, college-preparatory American literature class; and a tenth-grade composition course. Questions for this interview asked teachers how they might organize the course, what problems they might anticipate students having, what materials they might use, and what their goals would be for students. For two of the courses, teachers were given specific textbooks to critique and, in one case, to choose between. For the literature courses, teachers were given a hypothetical bookroom list (see Appendix C) from which to choose texts for their classes.

A fifth interview was added to this study when I discovered I would not have the chance to observe one of the teachers teach. Because I wanted the opportunity to collect some data on classroom practices, I decided to include a retrospective interview on the teaching of Shakespeare; five of the six teachers, including the one who had left teaching, taught a Shakespeare play sometime during their first year. This interview allowed me to gather data on how the teachers had planned and taught a full unit of instruction, as well as their evaluations and reflections on the unit; the interview also probed for the reasons behind their decisions and for their ideas about how they might teach the same material again to different types of students.

In addition to these five semi-structured interviews, the data for the case studies also included classroom observation of five of the six teachers. In most instances, I tried to observe a discrete unit of instruction; as several units lasted for three weeks, I was unable to observe the entire unit, but tried to observe several days at the beginning, several days in the middle, and several days at the end of the unit. I observed five of the teachers teach for at least four hours. As my interest was knowledge of teaching English, and not more general pedagogical knowledge, I did not focus on management issues in the teachers' classrooms. Field notes from the observations recorded teachers' explanations of topics and assignments, their use of metaphors or representations, their references to student understanding, and their responses to student questions and comments. The observations, then, focused particularly on the verbal interactions between teachers and students regarding the content of instruction.

In addition to the data collected on the individual teachers, I collected data on the teacher education program from which three of the teachers graduated. The central strategy for data collection was nonparticipant observation of the curriculum and instruction courses in English. I observed roughly half of the sessions of the two-quarter sequence of the curriculum and instruction class and obtained notes taken by one of the supervisors/teaching assistants of the class for the sessions I was unable to attend. I also collected all documents handed out to students in the course, such as booklists, syllabi, unit plans designed by students themselves, and copies of students' assignments. As most of the research on the influence of teacher education coursework has relied on self-report surveys filled out by instructors, I thought it essential to observe the courses that, theoretically, had the greatest opportunity to transmit pedagogical content knowledge. In addition to observation and document collection, I interviewed both the professor of English education and an English supervisor about the content of the courses as well as their goals for students.

A discontinuity exists in the data on the teacher education program, as I did not observe the curriculum and instruction classes during the actual quarters in which my informants were enrolled. Instead, I observed the courses during the year after these three teachers had graduated. The summer course was taught by the same professor both years; he was assisted by two of the same English supervisors during both years. According to one of the supervisors, the general content and structure of the course remained relatively stable. The fall course in the teaching of literature taken by my informants was taught by the same professor of English education, while during the quarter I observed the class, one of the supervisors taught the course. While the supervisor indicated that he based his version of the course very much on his observations of the professor's original course, the supervisor had his own style and preferences. For this reason, I concentrated primarily on the data from the summer curriculum and instruction course, using the data from the fall course more as a source of confirming and disconfirming evidence.

The lack of overlap between the actual courses taken by my informants and the courses I observed also meant that the mapping of influence focused more on general terrain than on specific features of the landscape. Occasionally, artifacts in the data prompted me to suspect the influence of the curriculum and instruction course, such as the finding that all three graduates selected *My Antonia* for their hypothetical course planning, without ever having read the book themselves. These artifacts, however, could not always be explained through analysis of the course data from the following year. In these instances, I interviewed an English supervisor who helped teach the course during both years about specific topics covered during the courses taken by my informants. She confirmed, for example, that *My Antonia* had been the topic of much discussion that year, because one of the teachers in this class had prepared a unit plan around the novel, which had been presented and distributed to the entire class. Interviews with this supervisor, then, helped me to account for some of the discontinuity in the data.

DATA ANALYSIS

The first stage of data analysis involved careful coding of all interview data. The coding categories, developed initially during the research on subject matter knowledge and then refined for the purposes of this study, included categories for both teacher knowledge and potential sources of teacher knowledge. Codes for teacher knowledge reflected the specific categories of pedagogical content knowledge, a general category for more generic pedagogical knowledge, and a general category for subject matter knowledge. Codes for the sources of teacher knowledge included: apprenticeship of observation as students (in which the emphasis was on pedagogical knowledge and skill); current and past teaching experience; other teachers; college and graduate work (in which the focus was on knowledge of content); teacher education coursework, subject-specific teacher education coursework, and teacher education fieldwork; in-service education and subject-specific in-service education; and other experience. This final coding scheme was refined again during the coding of the first set of data, and decision rules were documented and occasionally served as the topics for conceptual memos.

To check the reliability of my coding, I asked two researchers familiar with the general coding categories to code interview data from this study and then analyzed the extent to which our judgments concurred; inter-rater reliability was over 90 percent. The reliability of the coding in general was no doubt enhanced by our experience coding similar data from the Knowledge Growth project in a group setting. During these group coding efforts, we discussed, debated, and refined our coding categories until we were able to reach general consensus. After coding each set of interviews, I counted the number of attributions for each category of knowledge according to each source of knowledge, and compiled the results into charts of attributions of sources of knowledge for each individual teacher.

After each interview was coded, I summarized the content and general themes of the interview in a standard format. These analytic summaries served both as a strategy to reduce the overwhelming amount of data and as stimuli for further analysis of the data. I tried to include pertinent quotations and remarks of the teachers in the body of the summaries, as well as my tentative reactions and hypotheses in a concluding section. Occasionally, the final section would be the stimulus for a conceptual memo (Miles & Huberman, 1984). The summaries, then, became an analytic strategy both to preserve and to begin to interpret the rich qualitative data of the interviews.

In order to remain true to the intent of case study research, I analyzed all the data for each individual at one time. Once all the interviews and observations were summarized and the interview data were coded for a particular teacher, I wrote the first draft of a case study on the teacher. Again, the case study served as a data reduction technique, as I was able to preserve quotations and remarks, as well as an analytic tool. The purpose of the case study was to provide an in-depth portrait of each teacher, with as much salient data as possible, and to interpret the case with reference to the research questions of this study. By including many of the teachers' own words in these case studies, I wanted to offer the reader a chance to make alternative interpretations based on the actual data.

The second level of analysis involved cross-case analysis. After completing the preliminary analysis of the first three sets of data on the teachers without teacher education, I looked for patterns and themes common to all three cases and then summarized these themes in a lengthy conceptual memo. I followed the same procedure after completing the analysis of the three graduates of teacher education. I also aggregated the coded data into two overall charts, depicting the sources of different categories of pedagogical content knowledge for each group.

The third level of analysis, also involving cross-case analysis, looked across the two groups of teachers for patterns and themes related to the teachers' pedagogical content knowledge and its sources. While working on this level of cross-case analysis, I often referred to the interview summaries, individual case studies, and cross-case memos, looking for both confirming and disconfirming evidence. I created different tables and displays of the data to test my interpretations. For example, as I began to look more closely at the data on teachers' curricular knowledge, I found new ways of displaying and analyzing teachers' choices of texts. In analyzing the teachers' choices of texts, I asked two additional people to code the bookroom list texts as either canonical or adolescent works. One person was a professor of English and English education; the other was an experienced English teacher and graduate student. Inter-rater reliability on this coding exceeded 90 percent. These displays then revealed new or different patterns in the data, which provided disconfirming evidence to my earlier analyses, thus stimulating further analysis and interpretation.

This description of the cross-case analysis confirms the iterative nature of qualitative data analysis (Miles & Huberman, 1984). Data that seemed unimportant or trivial during an initial stage of analysis later became more consequential as the analysis progressed. The recursive process of data analysis also argues for a meticulously maintained and carefully catalogued database of qualitative data.

A separate stage of analysis was conducted on the teacher education data. Again, I summarized each observation both to reduce the raw data and to stimulate analysis. Fieldnotes from the observations of teacher education coursework were also coded with references to both the content and processes of instruction. Content codes included the categories of pedagogical content knowledge, theoretical concepts, practical suggestions, comments regarding the relationship of theory to practice, and references to the tradition of the teaching of English. Process codes included modeling, reflexive teaching, collegiality, and instances of instructional scaffolding.

Throughout the process of data analysis, I relied on conceptual memos as an analytic technique. As Miles and Huberman (1984) suggest, "Memos are always *conceptual* in intent. They do not just report data, but they tie different pieces of data together in a cluster, or they show that a particular piece of data is an instance of a general concept" (p. 69). Memos for this study were written both during the process of data collection and during data analysis. During data collection, memos served to record and discuss teachers' approaches to tasks or responses that seemed puzzling or theoretically significant at the time. For example, while conducting the interviews on simulated planning, I noted that two of the graduates of teacher education seemed to have relatively low expectations for students, as evidenced by the overlap of texts chosen for a ninth-grade, general-track class and an eleventh-grade, college-preparatory class. I also commented on the differences between the general "types" of texts chosen by Megan and Steven, on the one hand, and Lance and Jake, on the other. While these early memos recorded my impressions, they did not attempt to interpret the data in much depth. Later memos, written during the process of data analysis when I had access to the entire body of data, were more analytic.

Attempts to display the qualitative data also emerged as an analytic technique in this study (Miles & Huberman, 1984). Displays of data uncovered missing data; when I developed a chart that listed each teacher's motivation for teaching, conception of English, and general conception of teaching, I discovered that I could not fill in the cell for "general conception of teaching" for the three graduates of teacher education. After going back to the original interview data, I found that for these teachers, their conceptions of teaching seemed inextricably tied to their conceptions of teaching English. In the iterative nature of qualitative data analysis, a gap in the data display sent me back to the data and eventually caused me to rethink my conceptual framework. The displays of data also revealed patterns that did not emerge in initial analyses. In my analysis of the interview involving simulated planning, I constructed charts that listed each teacher's goals, expectations, organization, and choices of texts for each course. From these displays, I concluded that the nature of texts chosen by the teachers seemed, intuitively, important. I then generated more charts that displayed the choices of texts in a variety of ways; not until the third and fourth generations of charts did I see that the patterns differed for ninth-grade English and American literature. While I always had felt quite comfortable relying on narrative accounts of qualitative data, this study made me realize the value of other techniques for displaying data. (See Miles and Huberman, 1984 for a discussion of possible formats for displaying qualitative data.)

INTERACTIVE ISSUES

As is true of all research that involves interaction between people, some of the methodological concerns in this study revolve around the interaction between researcher and informants (Georges & Jones, 1980). My particular methodological concerns had to do with the expectations of the first-year teachers with whom I worked and my role as a researcher; while I had confronted some of the issues arising from the human aspect of research in prior studies of beginning teachers, this aspect of conducting research deserves scrutiny, for both methodological and ethical reasons.

While I had anticipated difficulty finding first-year teachers willing to participate in a study that would necessarily consume their time and attention during an already exhausting experience, the people I contacted all agreed to be in the study. The graduates of teacher education, whom I already knew through my role as a teaching assistant in a required teacher education course, saw the research as a chance to continue their interest in inquiries regarding teaching; two of the three had participated in another research project the year before. They also indicated to me that they appreciated having someone observe their teaching. As Vanessa suggested to me, "You forget why you're doing what you're doing." While the teachers seemed to enjoy having someone to talk with, they also may have expected me to give them feedback about their teaching; their implicit model of an observer in their classrooms was their supervisor from the teacher education program. While I clearly differentiated my role from that of a supervisor, I also said that once the research was completed, we could talk about their teaching, if they so desired. None of the graduates of teacher education took me up on this offer, an indication that they were willing to accept my role solely as that of a researcher; this interpretation was supported when I received a call from Vanessa telling me about an opportunity to do further research on this same topic at her school.

The other concern I had about the participation of the graduates of professional preparation had to do with my prior relationship with them as their teaching assistant. Because I was not affiliated with the subject-specific components of the program, this prior relationship did not develop into as serious a source of potential bias as it might have been. Nonetheless, I took our prior relationship into account when I analyzed the data concerning the course in which I had assisted. The most obvious effect of this prior relationship was their assumption that since I knew the content of that course, they did not have to elaborate on what they learned.

While the graduates of teacher education were used to having observers in their classrooms, the teachers without teacher education were not. Participating in this research meant opening their classroom door to a relative stranger. Part of my reason for delaying classroom observation, particularly for Kate and Jake, had to do with the need to establish a relationship prior to observation. While both of them still felt apprehensive about my observations, they were extremely gracious in allowing me to observe whenever I could. As Jake felt that the class I had chosen to observe was not representative of his teaching in general, I observed both his freshman class and his senior class.

While I made it clear that I was not there to supervise their teaching, I also made them the same promise I had made the other teachers; once the research was finished, we could get together to talk about their teaching. Kate took me up on the offer, and we met for lunch. After talking about her strengths and a few areas for improvement, I told her some of my emerging findings, which she seemed to accept. Jake did not take me up on my offer.

As a researcher, I tried to develop an opaque facade, attempting to be supportive, but noncommittal. The twin of opacity, however, is reflection. I found that the informants saw in me what they wanted to see, which usually involved a mirror image of their own concerns. The graduates of teacher education assumed that I supported the philosophy of teaching English underlying their professional preparation; they saw in me an experienced English teacher with an affiliation to their teacher education program. The teachers without teacher education paid more attention to my credentials as an English major with an educational and disciplinary background similar to their own. As I analyzed the data, I tried to find comments about how the teachers saw the nature of our relationship, and how that interpretation may have colored what they told me.

APPENDIX B

Interview Protocols

INTERVIEW #1
Knowledge/Conceptions of English and Teaching English

Introduction: First I'll be talking to you as someone who knows about the field of English, and we'll be talking a little bit about your undergraduate and graduate background in English. At this point, we won't be talking about teaching English, but rather the study of English as a discipline.

1. Can you tell me about your background in English?
    Tell me about your courses.
        undergraduate and graduate
        favorite and least favorite
    What areas did you concentrate on? specialization?
    What do you feel are your strengths in English?
    What areas do you feel relatively weak in?
    What areas were easy for you? difficult?
    Tell me about some of the most important English papers
        you wrote as an undergraduate.

2. What do you think it means for someone to know English? If someone is a self-proclaimed expert in English, what would you expect them to know?

3. Could you talk about the major areas that make up English as a field or discipline? Tell me how the areas are related to each other. (Could you draw a map of the different areas and their relationships?)

4. Now I'd like to talk to you as an English teacher. What made you decide to become an English teacher? [probe for both reasons for teaching and reasons for teaching English]

5. Tell me about what you see as the reasons for studying English in high school. What are your goals for your students? What areas would you want to cover in your classes? [probe for conceptions of teaching both literature and writing]

6. What do you think makes English difficult for students? What areas do you think they might have problems with? What is easy for high school students? What could make the study of English easier for students? [probe for both literature and writing]

7. Tell me about the classes you are teaching this semester. How are the classes organized? What books or units are you teaching? Are you familiar with these books? Have you read them before? Have you taught them before? Tell me about the students in your classes.

INTERVIEW #2
Transcript-Guided Interview

1. I have written out the names of the courses you took in college [and graduate school]. Could you first sort the cards according to how they influenced how you think about English? How did they influence your understanding of English as a discipline?

2. Now could you sort the cards according to how they influenced your ideas about how to teach English? How did they influence your ideas about teaching English? [probe for both positive and negative influences]

3. Tell me about any other experiences you have had that have affected how you think about teaching English.

4. Tell me about the best and worst teacher you ever had.

For teacher education graduates only

5. Here are the titles of courses that you took during your year of teacher preparation. Could you sort them into categories that are meaningful to you? How have you grouped them? Tell me about each pile. Are there other ways you might group them? Tell me about the different ways.

6. Let's go through the titles one by one and talk about what you got out of each one. [Probe for both coursework and fieldwork]

INTERVIEW #3
Teaching a Common Text

This interview uses the poem "The Death of the Ball Turret Gunner" by Randall Jarrell. First, have informants read the poem through to themselves.

From my mother's sleep I fell into the State,
And I hunched in its belly till my wet fur froze.
Six miles from earth, loosed from its dream of life,

I woke to black flak and the nightmare fighters.
When I died they washed me out of the turret with a hose.

1. Could you talk a little bit about this poem? Tell me what you think the poem is about. If you were talking about the poem to a fellow English major, what might you say? [probe for what they might do in order to understand the poem better]

2. As you read through the poem again, think about teaching it to a junior or senior English class. Could you talk about some of the things you might think about in preparing to teach this poem? What are some of your first thoughts about teaching this poem?

3. What would your goals be for teaching this poem? What would you want students to get out of it?

4. How might you use this poem in a course? What units might you use it with? [probe for different ways they might use the poem]

5. Can you tell me about some of the activities you might use in teaching this poem? What kind of assignments would you use with this poem?

6. Tell me about the difficulties you might expect students to have with this poem. How do you think they would respond to this poem? What difficulties do you think students have with poetry in general? How might you help them overcome these problems?

7. Let's say you're teaching this poem to a class, and one of your students asks you the following questions. Respond to me as you might to a student asking these questions. [clarify this as role-playing situation]

a. Why is this a poem? I thought poems were supposed to rhyme.
b. People don't have fur. Why is this person talking about wet fur freezing?
c. What is "loosed from its dream of life"? I don't get it!
d. How do we know that what we're saying about this poem is right? Maybe the guy just had a nightmare or something and it doesn't mean anything at all.
e. I still don't get this poem! What's the message anyway, and why couldn't he just tell us in plain English?

8. After teaching this poem to a class, how would you evaluate their understanding of it? How might you find out what they had gotten out of the poem?

9. Here are three different texts that contain this poem. Look over the section that contains the poem and the questions and materials that accompany the poem. Which of these texts would you be most likely to use? Least likely? Why? Tell me about your reactions to these texts.

Texts include: *Understanding Poetry*, edited by C. Brooks and R. P. Warren (Holt, Rinehart, & Winston); *The Lyric Voice: Poetry*, edited by A.

R. Kitzhaber, S. Malarkey, & B. Drake (Holt, Rinehart and Winston); *Adventures in American Literature*, edited by R. B. Inglis (Harcourt, Brace).

INTERVIEW #4
Planning for Courses

You've just been told by your principal that you have to take over an ailing colleague's classes. You will start in a week, so you don't have much time to prepare before the school year starts. You'll be teaching a general-track, freshman class, a composition course for tenth graders, and a college-preparatory, American literature class for eleventh graders. We'll be talking about each of these courses one by one. Which one would you feel most comfortable about starting with? [go over list of courses again; start with the one chosen and then go through all three classes] [clarify that they will be taking over at the beginning of year; classes will not have met yet, so they can start from the beginning of the year]

1. Tell me about your initial thoughts about teaching this class. How would you feel about teaching such a class? What general concerns might you have?
2. What would your goals be for your students in this class?
3. Tell me how you might organize the course. Why? What other ways might you think about organizing it?
4. What would you expect students to know about the topics in this class? Tell me about the topics or areas you would expect students to have problems with. Why?
5. What books or materials would you think about using for this class? [probe for both titles and reasons for choices]
6. Your department chair has just handed you the textbooks and bookroom list for your classes. You have a choice of composition texts: *Writer's Workshop* or *Composition and Grammar*. For American literature, the assigned text is *Adventures in American Literature*. The ninth-grade class has no assigned textbook. You will be choosing from the bookroom list.

For composition course

a. Which text would you be more likely to use? Why? Tell me what you think about each text.
b. Tell me how you might use the text for class.
c. Tell me about the strengths and weaknesses of each text.
d. Do you have a text in mind that you would prefer to use? What is it? Tell me why you would prefer it.

For American literature course

a. After looking through the text, tell me what you think of it. How might you use the text?
b. You can supplement the text with books from the bookroom. Here is the list [see Appendix C]. Which texts would you want to use in your course? Why have you chosen these?
c. You've just been told you can order two texts of your own choosing. Which might you add to this course? Which books would you get rid of?

For ninth-grade English

a. You have no assigned textbook for this course. You can choose your texts from this bookroom list. Look through the list again and choose the books you would want to use for this class. Tell me about why you have chosen these texts. How might you use them in the course?
b. You've just been told you can order two texts of your own choosing, any two you want. What books might you choose to add to this course? Which books would you get rid of?

INTERVIEW #5
Retrospective Interview on Teaching a Unit

[Whenever possible, have this interview focus on teaching Shakespeare.]

1. Tell me about your unit on ________.
   How did you introduce it?
   What were your goals for the unit?
   What kinds of things did you take into consideration in planning the unit?
   Can you tell me about some of the discussions/lessons?
   How long did the unit take?
   Was the text required by your school or did you choose it?
   If you chose it, why did you choose this text?
2. Tell me about the students in the class. [probe for number of students, heterogeneity or homogeneity of class]
3. Tell me about any assignments or activities that you used in the unit. Do you have any copies I could see?
4. Did you have any final paper or test associated with the unit? What was it like?
5. Tell me what you thought the students got out of the unit.

6. Tell me how you thought the unit went. How would you change the unit if you were to teach it again?

7. How might you change the unit if you were teaching a much stronger group of students? How about for a weaker group of students?

APPENDIX C

Bookroom List

The Scarlet Letter
Spoon River Anthology
A Separate Peace
Portrait of the Artist as a Young Man
The Old Man and the Sea
The Sound and the Fury
Cannery Row
The Contender
Catcher in the Rye
Norton Anthology of Poetry
Julius Caesar
The Grapes of Wrath
Points of View (short story anthology)
Introduction to the Short Story
Walden
The Crucible
Great Expectations
To Kill a Mockingbird
The Unvanquished
Paradise Lost
Hamlet
Native Son
The Last of the Mohicans
My Antonia
Dandelion Wine
Things Fall Apart
Jane Eyre
Who's Afraid of Virginia Woolf
The Awakening
The Woman Warriors
The Outsiders
Long Day's Journey into Night
Fahrenheit 451
A Farewell to Arms
Moby Dick
Billy Budd and Other Stories
King Lear
A Streetcar Named Desire
Black Boy
Pride and Prejudice
Animal Farm
Reflections on a Gift of Watermelon Pickle
Death of a Salesman
The Adventures of Huckleberry Finn
Warriner's Grammar and Composition, Grade Nine
Writer's Workshop
Vocabulary for the High School Student
Vocabulary for the College Bound Student

References

Adelman, N. E. (1986). *An exploratory study of teacher alternative certification and retraining programs*. Washington, DC: Policy Studies Associates.

Ammon, P. (1988, April). *Regression and progression in teachers' pedagogical conceptions*. Paper presented at the annual meeting of the American Educational Research Association, New Orleans.

Applebee, A. N. (1974). *Tradition and reform in the teaching of English*. Urbana, IL: National Council of Teachers of English.

Ball, D. L. (1990, April). *Becoming a mathematics teacher through college-based and alternate routes*. Paper presented at the annual meeting of the American Educational Research Association, Boston.

Ball, D. L. (1988). *Knowledge and reasoning in mathematical pedagogy: Examining what prospective teachers bring with them to teacher education*. Unpublished doctoral dissertation, College of Education, Michigan State University, East Lansing.

Barnes, H. L. (1987). The conceptual basis for thematic teacher education programs. *Journal of Teacher Education, 38* (4), 13–18.

Baxter, J., Richert, A., & Saylor, C. (1985). *Content and process in biology* (Knowledge Growth in a Profession Technical Report). Stanford, CA: School of Education, Stanford University.

Braddock, R. (1963). *Research in written composition*. Urbana, IL: National Council of Teachers of English.

Byrne, C. J. (1983, October). *Teacher knowledge and teacher effectiveness: A literature review, theoretical analysis, and discussion of research strategy*. Paper presented at the 14th Annual Convention of the Northeastern Educational Research Association, Ellenville, NY.

Carlsen, W. S. (1988). *The effects of science teacher subject-matter knowledge on teacher questioning and classroom discourse*. Unpublished doctoral dissertation, Stanford University, Stanford, CA.

Carpenter, T. P., Fennema, E., Peterson, P. L., & Carey, D. A. (1988). Teachers' pedagogical content knowledge of students' problem solving in elementary arithmetic. *Journal for Research in Mathematics Education, 19* (5), 385–401.

Carroll, J. B. (1963). A model for school learning. *Teachers College Record, 64* (8), 723–733.

Clark, C. M., & Peterson, P. L. (1986). Teachers' thought processes. In M. C. Wittrock (Ed.), *Handbook of research on teaching* (3rd ed., pp. 255–296). New York: Macmillan.

Cohen, D. (1986). *Assessing the quality of teacher education*. East Lansing, MI: National Center for Research on Teacher Education.

Conant, J. (1963). *The education of American teachers*. New York: McGraw-Hill.

Cronbach, L. J. (1966). The logic of experiments on discovery. In L. S. Shulman & E. R. Keislar (Eds.), *Learning by discovery: A critical appraisal* (pp. 75–92). Chicago: Rand McNally.

Cuban, L. (1984). *How teachers taught: Constancy and change in American classrooms: 1890–1980*. New York: Longman.

Dewey, J. (1902/1983). The child and the curriculum. In J. A. Boydston (Ed.), *John Dewey: The middle works, 1899–1924: Volume 2: 1902–1903*. Carbondale, IL: Southern Illinois University Press.

Doyle, W. (1986). Classroom organization and management. In M. C. Wittrock (Ed.), *Handbook of research on teaching* (3rd ed., pp. 392–431). New York: Macmillan.

Edmundson, P. J. (1989, August). *The curriculum in teacher education* (Study of the Education of Educators Technical Report #6). Center for Educational Renewal, University of Washington, Seattle.

Education secretary says let those who can, teach. (1986, July 15). *San Francisco Chronicle*, p. 15.

Einhorn, H. J. (1980). Learning from experience and suboptimal rules in decision making. In T. S. Wallsten (Ed.), *Cognitive processes in choice and decision behavior*. Hillsdale, N.J.: Lawrence Erlbaum.

Elbaz, F. (1983). *Teacher thinking: A study of practical knowledge*. New York: Nichols Publishing Company.

Elley, W. B., Barham, I. H., Lamb, H., & Wyllie, M. (1979). *The role of grammar in a secondary school curriculum*. Christchurch, New Zealand: New Zealand Council for Educational Research.

Emig, J. (1971). *The composing processes of twelfth graders*. Urbana, IL: National Council of Teachers of English.

Fagan, E. R., & Laine, C. H. (1980). Two perspectives on undergraduate English teacher preparation. *Research in the Teaching of English, 14* (1), 67–72.

Feiman-Nemser, S. (Ed.). (1987). *Teacher education and learning to teach: Proceedings of the First Annual NCRTE Retreat*. (Conference Series 87–1). East Lansing, MI: National Center for Research on Teacher Education.

Feiman-Nemser, S. (1983). Learning to teach. In L. S. Shulman & G. Sykes (Eds.), *Handbook of teaching and policy* (pp. 150–170). New York: Longman.

Feiman-Nemser, S., & Amarel, M. (1988, April). *Prospective teachers' views of learning to teach*. Paper presented at the annual meeting of the American Educational Research Association, New Orleans.

Feiman-Nemser, S., & Buchmann, M. (1985). Pitfalls of experience in teacher preparation. *Teachers College Record, 87* (1), 53–65.

Gage, N. L. (1978). *The scientific basis of the art of teaching*. New York: Teachers College Press.

Gantner, K. K. (1978). *A comprehensive survey of the status of English methods courses in New England colleges and universities*. Unpublished doctoral dissertation, Boston University. DAI, *39*, 2876A.

Georges, R. A., & Jones, M. L. (1980). *People studying people: The human element in fieldwork*. Berkeley: University of California Press.

Gomez, M. L. (1990, April). *Learning to teach writing in college-based and alternate route programs of teacher education*. Paper presented at the annual meeting of the American Educational Research Association, Boston.

Gomez, M. L. (1988, April). *Prospective teachers' beliefs about good writing*. Paper presented at the annual meeting of the American Educational Research Association, New Orleans.

Goodlad, J. (1988). Studying the education of educators: A value-driven inquiry. *Phi Delta Kappan, 70* (2), 104–111.

Grant, G. (1987, April). *Pedagogical content knowledge: A case study of four secondary teachers*. Paper presented at the annual meeting of the American Educational Research Association, Washington, DC.

Griffin, G. A. (1986). Clinical teacher education. In J. V. Hoffman & S. A. Edwards (Eds.), *Reality and reform in clinical teacher education* (pp. 1–23). New York: Random House.

Grommon, A. H. (1984). Why look back? *English Journal*, March, 26–29.

Grossman, P. L. (in press). What are we talking about anyhow? Subject matter knowledge of English teachers. In J. Brophy (Ed.), *Advances in research on teaching, Second Volume*. JAI Press.

Grossman, P. L. (1987). *Conviction—that granitic base: The case study of Martha, a beginning English teacher*. Knowledge Growth in a Profession Technical Report. Stanford, CA: School of Education, Stanford University.

Grossman, P. L., & Gudmundsdottir, S. (1987, April). *Teachers and texts: An expert/novice study in English*. Paper presented at the annual meeting of the American Educational Research Association, Washington, DC.

Grossman, P. L., & Richert, A. E. (1988). Unacknowledged knowledge growth: A re-examination of the effects of teacher education. *Teaching and Teacher Education: An International Journal of Research and Studies, 4* (1), 53–62.

Grossman, P. L., & Wilson, S. M. (1987, April). *Planting seeds: The use of case studies in the generation and elaboration of educational theory*. Paper presented at the annual meeting of the American Educational Research Association, Washington, DC.

Grossman, P. L., Wilson, S. M., & Shulman, L. S. (1989). Teachers of substance: Subject matter knowledge for teaching. In M. Reynolds (Ed.), *Knowledge base for the beginning teacher* (pp. 23–36). New York: Pergamon.

Grunska, G. P. (1978). *A study of English methods courses in selected midwestern colleges*. Unpublished doctoral dissertation, Northwestern University. DAI, *39*, 4692A.

Gudmundsdottir, S. (1989). *Knowledge use among experienced teachers: Four case studies of high school teaching*. Unpublished doctoral dissertation, Stanford University, Stanford, CA.

Hashweh, M. Z. (1987). Effects of subject matter knowledge in teaching biology and physics. *Teaching and Teacher Education: An International Journal of Research and Studies, 3* (2), 109–120.

Hipple, T. W. (1974). What goes on in the English methods course? *English Education, 5* (4), 225–237.

Holmes Group. (1986). *Tomorrow's teachers: A report of the Holmes group*. East Lansing, MI: Holmes Group.

Houston, W. R. (1983). Teacher education programs. In H. E. Mitzel (Ed.), *Encyclopedia of educational research* (5th ed., pp. 1881–1891). New York: The Free Press.

Howsam, R. B., Corrigan, D. C., Denemark, G. W., & Nash, R. J. (1976). *Educating a profession*. Washington, DC: American Association of Colleges for Teacher Education.

Jackson, P. (1986). *The practice of teaching*. New York: Teachers College Press.

Katz, L., & Raths, J. (1988, April). *Dilemmas in teacher education*. Paper presented at the annual meeting of the American Educational Research Association, New Orleans.

Katz, L., & Raths, J. (1982). The best of intentions for the education of teachers. *Action in Teacher Education, 4* (1), 8–16.

Kerr, D. H. (1983). Teaching competence and teacher education in the United States. *Teachers College Record, 84* (3), 525–552.

Kerr, D. H. (1981). The structure of quality in teaching. In J. Soltis (Ed.), *Philosophy and education* (80th yearbook of the National Society for the Study of Education). Chicago: University of Chicago Press.

Koerner, J. D. (1963). *The miseducation of American teachers*. Boston: Houghton Mifflin.

Lamme, L. L., & Ross, D. D. (1981). Graduate methods classes: Do they influence teaching methods? *Journal of Teacher Education, 32* (6), 25–29.

Lampert, M. (1984). Teaching about thinking and thinking about teaching. *Journal of Curriculum Studies, 16* (1), 1–18.

Langer, J. A., & Applebee, A. N. (1986). Reading and writing instruction: Toward a theory of teaching and learning. In E. Z. Rothkopf (Ed.), *Review of research in education, Vol. 13* (pp. 171–194). Washington, DC: American Educational Research Association.

Lanier, J. E., & Little, J. W. (1986). Research on teacher education. In M. C. Wittrock (Ed.), *Handbook of research on teaching* (3rd ed., pp. 527–569). New York: Macmillan.

Lawrenz, F., & Cohen, H. (1985). The effect of methods classes and practice teaching on student attitudes toward science and knowledge of science processes. *Science Education, 69* (1), 105–113.

Leinhardt, G., & Smith, D. (1985). Expertise in mathematics instruction: Subject matter knowledge. *Journal of Educational Psychology, 77* (3), 247–271.

Little, J. W. (1982). Norms of collegiality and experimentation: Workplace conditions of school success. *American Educational Research Journal, 19*, 325–340.

Lortie, D. C. (1975). *Schoolteacher: A sociological study*. Chicago: University of Chicago Press.

Lundgren, U. P. (1972). *Frame factors and the teaching process*. Stockholm: Elmquist & Wiksell.

McCaleb, J. L. (1979). On reconciling dissonance between preparation and practice. *Journal of Teacher Education, 30* (4), 50–53.

McDiarmid, G. W. (1989). *Understanding history for teaching: A plan of study*. Unpublished manuscript, Michigan State University.

McDiarmid, G. W., Ball, D. L., & Anderson, C. W. (1989). Why staying one chapter ahead doesn't really work: Subject-specific pedagogy. In M. C. Reynolds (Ed.), *Knowledge base for the beginning teacher* (pp. 193–206). New York: Pergamon.

McEvoy, B. C. (1984). *Behind closed doors: A study of curriculum stability*. Unpublished doctoral dissertation, Stanford University, Stanford, CA.

McEwan, H. (1987). *Interpreting the subject domains for students: Towards a rhetorical theory of teaching*. Unpublished doctoral dissertation, University of Washington, Seattle.

Miles, M. B., & Huberman, A. M. (1984). *Qualitative data analysis: A sourcebook of new methods*. Beverly Hills, CA: Sage.

Natriello, G., Zumwalt, K., Hansen, A., & Frisch, A. (1988, April). *Who is choosing alternative routes into teaching?* Paper presented at the annual meeting of the American Educational Research Association, New Orleans.

Nespor, J. (1987). The role of beliefs in the practice of teaching. *Journal of Curriculum Studies, 19* (4), 317–328.

O'Donnell, R. C. (1979). Research in the teaching of English: Some observations and questions. *English Education, 10* (3), 181–182.

Oftedahl, J. L. (1985). Secondary English methods courses in the Midwest. *English Education, 17* (3), 153–161.

Quisenberry, J. D. (1981). English teacher preparation: What's happening? *English Education, 13* (2), 70–77.

Ravitch, D., & Finn, C. E. (1987). *What do our 17-year-olds know?* New York: Harper & Row.

Reynolds, M. C. (1989). *Knowledge base for the beginning teacher*. New York: Pergamon Press.

Reynolds, J. A., Haymore, J., Ringstaff, C., & Grossman, P. L. (1988). Teachers and curriculum materials: Who is driving whom? *Curriculum Perspectives, 8* (1), 22–30.

Richert, A. E. (in press). Teaching teachers to reflect: A consideration of program structure. *Journal of Curriculum Studies*.

Ringstaff, C. (1989). *Teacher misassignment: A matter of degrees*. Unpublished doctoral dissertation, Stanford University, Stanford, CA.

Rodman, B. (1988, February 24). "Alternate route" said a success. *Education Week*, p. 7.

Rorro, C. (1987, April). *New Jersey's provisional teacher program: An alternative route to certification*. Paper presented at the annual meeting of the American Educational Research Association, Washington, DC.

Rowe, M. B. (1974). Wait time and rewards as instructional variables, their influence on language, logic, and fate control: Part I: Wait time. *Journal of Research in Science Teaching, 11*, 81–94.

Sarason, S. B., Davidson, K. R., & Blatt, B. (1962). *The preparation of teachers*. New York: John Wiley.

Schlechty, P. C., & Vance, V. S. (1983). Recruitment, selection, and retention: The shape of the teaching force. *Elementary School Journal, 83*, 469–487.

Schön, D. (1983). *The reflective practitioner*. New York: Basic Books.

Schwab, J. J. (1964). The structure of disciplines: Meanings and significance. In G. W. Ford & L. Pugno (Eds.), *The structure of knowledge and the curriculum*. Chicago: Rand McNally.

Shavelson, R. J., & Stern, P. (1981). Research on teachers' pedagogical thoughts, judgments, decisions, and behaviors. *Review of Educational Research, 51*, 455–498.

Shulman, J. (1989). Blue freeways: Traveling the alternate route with big-city teacher trainees. *Journal of Teacher Education, 40* (5), 2–8.

Shulman, L. S. (1987). Knowledge and teaching: Foundations of the new reform. *Harvard Educational Review, 57* (1), 1–22.

Shulman, L. S. (1986a). Those who understand: Knowledge growth in teaching. *Educational Researcher, 15* (2), 4–14.

Shulman, L. S. (1986b). Paradigms and research programs in the study of teaching: A contemporary perspective. In M. C. Wittrock (Ed.), *Handbook of research on teaching* (3rd ed., pp. 3–36). New York: Macmillan.

Shulman, L. S. (1983). Autonomy and obligation: The remote control of teaching. In L. S. Shulman & G. Sykes (Eds.), *Handbook of teaching and policy*. New York: Longman.

Shulman, L. S., & Grossman, P. L. (1987). *Final report to the Spencer Foundation* (Technical Report of the Knowledge Growth in a Profession Research Project). Stanford, CA: School of Education, Stanford University.

Smith, J., & Hickman, R. (1978). The impact of a foundations of education course on attitudes: Results of a longitudinal study. *Educational and Psychological Measurement, 38*, 761–770.

Steinberg, R., Marks, R., & Haymore, J. (1985). *Teachers' knowledge and structuring of content in mathematics* (Knowledge Growth in a Profession Technical Report). Stanford, CA: School of Education, Stanford University.

Stoddard, T. (1988, April). *Nonlinear patterns of development: Implications for research on teacher thinking*. Paper presented at the annual meeting of the American Educational Research Association, New Orleans.

Tversky, A., & Kahneman, D. (1974). Judgment under uncertainty: Heuristics and biases. *Science, 185*, 1124–1131.

Vance, V. S., & Schlechty, P. C. (1982). The distribution of academic ability in the teaching force: Policy implications. *Phi Delta Kappan, 64* (1), 2–27.

Veenman, S. (1984). Perceived problems of beginning teachers. *Review of Educational Research, 54* (2), 143–178.

Wilson, S. M. (1988). *Representations of knowledge in teaching: A case of American history*. Unpublished doctoral dissertation, Stanford University, Stanford, CA.

Wilson, S. M., & Wineburg, S. S. (1988). Peering at history through different lenses: The role of disciplinary perspectives in teaching history. *Teachers College Record, 89*, 525–539.

Wilson, S. M., Shulman, L. S., & Richert, A. E. (1987). "150 different ways" of knowing: Representations of knowledge in teaching. In J. Calderhead (Ed.), *Exploring teachers' thinking* (pp. 104–124). London: Cassell.

Wineburg, S. S., & Wilson, S. M. (in press). Subject matter knowledge in the teaching of American history. In J. Brophy (Ed.), *Advances in research on teaching, second volume*. JAI Press.

Wineburg, S. S. (1990). *Historical problem solving: A study of the cognitive processes used in the evaluation of documentary evidence*. Unpublished doctoral dissertation, Stanford University, Stanford, CA.

Yin, R. K. (1984). *Case study research: Design and methods*. Beverly Hills, CA: Sage.

Zeichner, K. M. (1988, April). *Understanding the character and quality of the academic and professional components of teacher education*. Paper presented at the annual meeting of the American Educational Research Association, New Orleans.

Zeichner, K. M., & Tabachnik, B. R. (1981). Are the effects of teacher education "washed out" by school experience? *Journal of Teacher Education, 32* (3), 7–11.

Zumwalt, K. K. (1982). Research on teaching: Policy implications for teacher education. In A. Lieberman & M. W. McLaughlin (Eds.), *Policy making in education* (81st yearbook of the National Society for the Study of Education, Part 1, pp. 215–248). Chicago: University of Chicago Press.

Index

About the Author

Pamela L. Grossman is an assistant professor in the Department of Curriculum and Instruction at the University of Washington. She received a B.A. in English and a secondary teaching credential at Yale University and taught English in a variety of education settings, prior to obtaining her doctorate at Stanford University. She is currently engaged in creating a teacher education program through the Puget Sound Professional Development Center. Her research interests include the study of teacher knowledge and beliefs and the teacher education curriculum.